RISE

The science and practice of creating
and developing your cognitive resources
for resilience and wellbeing

DR SAM MATHER

Re think

First published in Great Britain in 2021
by Rethink Press (www.rethinkpress.com)

Cover image © Shutterstock | birulaut03

To my father, Ken Mather. I miss you and think of you every day. You gave me what I needed to be where I am. I hope this would have made you proud.

d. September 2019

Contents

Introduction

The world is changing, rapidly and unexpectedly. The way we live, work and socialise is different. The days of living and working in a local community has been replaced by the 'global village'. Social media has created cross country communities; the ability to live and work anywhere in the world is not only becoming easier but has become aspirational. Spending years working for the same company, working side-by-side with your colleagues has been replaced by shorter tenures, either through contractual changes or personal choice and international teams. Communication has become almost instantaneous, meaning that responses to new information are expected to be immediate. Add to this the complexity, stress and challenges of a global pandemic and life has become much bigger, faster and noisier. This is especially true for the workplace which has become, as a result, increasingly demanding. Organisations now operate in a VUCA environment – volatile, uncertain, complex and ambiguous – and our jobs are constantly changing. New challenges, such as technological and biological viruses, require leaders to work quickly on innovative solutions. Our workplaces are all intertwined, meaning something happening in one industry impacts another. It's getting more and more difficult to plan ahead. All these factors contribute to increasingly stressful workplaces for us all, and it's no surprise that mental health and well-being issues are becoming more prevalent.

Organisations are responding by providing support for employees through training and formal well-being programmes; however, if you're at the point where you have to be referred for resilience training or employee counselling, your cognitive resources have already depleted and your resilience has faltered. It would be better to prevent the need for these measures by understanding and taking control of the mechanisms that lead to a loss of resilience.

Think of your brain as a car engine. When you understand the mechanics, you can tweak it to increase its performance and resilience. Like a Haynes car manual, this book will provide checklists and instructions on getting the most out of your brain – only more fun and entertaining.

Based on research into the cognitive resources needed to maximise the brain's performance, this book offers simple metaphors, clear diagrams, questionnaires and step-by-step guides. We'll explore how amazingly clever and brilliant the brain is while at the same time being malevolent. Feed the brain the wrong food at the wrong time, and like a cute and loving mogwai it becomes a destructive gremlin. By understanding how the brain can help or harm you, you can begin to manage it and take control, helping you reach your potential and RISE above that which does not serve you.

Sometimes you have to remind your brain who is in charge (ie, you). In this book, I'll provide you with activities and exercises that teach you about yourself, show you how your brain works with (and against) you, and help you focus on what's important. By the end, you will have a toolkit to enable you to become SOUND and resilient.

What does being SOUND mean?

sound (*adj*) **1.** not broken or damaged, healthy or in good condition. **2.** showing or based on good judgement. **3.** complete or detailed. **4.** able to be trusted because of having a lot of ability or knowledge. **5.** not harmful or wrong[1]

A SOUND person is 'resource-full'. They create, build and maintain the right mental, emotional, and physical resources that they need and then deploy them in a way that is flexible, adaptable, innovative, smart, positive, self-aware, engaged and successful. Someone who is SOUND is able to do this in both good times and bad.

This may sound similar to resilience, defined as the process, or 'capacity for successful adaptation despite challenging or threatening circumstances',[2] which is considered to be a result of normal, basic human adaptation systems.[3] This normal adaptation system is generally effective – so effective, in fact, that our means of coping with stressors can make us ill.

For years, we can use all of our mental and physical resources to cope with stress, until the day we totally lose it. You react to something emotionally, losing your temper and control, lashing out at those you love, those you hate, random people you don't care about – and of course yourself. People who don't have adequate mental, emotional and physical resources are unable to process information fully, leading to negative attitudes, cynicism, emotional responses, and an inability to deal with anything new, different or unwanted.[4]

SOUND people go beyond responding reactively because they are resource-full. Being resource-full involves knowing themselves: which resources deplete them, making them feel bad, and which replenish them, making them feel good. They monitor their resource levels, and they actively seek and develop the resources they need when they need them. Having gained these resources, the SOUND adult chooses where to invest and deploy these resources. They use their resources to manage their environment, rather than their environment managing their resources.

SOUND individuals are able to manage their thoughts and emotions, recognising that these can use up resources unnecessarily. In understanding that the brain can work with or against them, they manage it accordingly, creating clarity of thought and rational responses. A SOUND person has the resources – and desire – to learn, grow and become better every day. They enable themselves to RISE: to be Resilient, Innovative, Shift and Evolve, allowing them to deal with whatever life throws at them.

The good news is that there are ways to become SOUND. Using research from neuroscience (science of the brain), psychology, physiology and biology, this book will provide you with skills to maintain your mental well-being and resilience in this complex world.

PART ONE
THE THEORY

Theory is not as dull as it sounds. This part of the book offers an easy-to-understand overview of how the brain works and affects our actions. By understanding how something works, you are in a better position to get the most out of it and improve its performance. I have a car and I use it every day. I know that I need to 'feed' it petrol (don't worry, the next one will be electric) and occasionally, when I remember, I give it oil and pump up the tyres. That is the sum total of my knowledge of how cars work. It's enough to get me where I need to go safely and maintain the life of the car – until something changes. A light on the dashboard comes on. The engine 'sounds funny' or it is slow to accelerate, or it simply doesn't start. The car's performance has deteriorated, and I have no idea why, so I can't do anything about it. I have to pay a fortune to a garage to find what may be a simple problem.

If I had better knowledge of the workings of a car, I might be able to fix the problem myself. I could tweak the engine, or gears, or whatever (see, I told you I knew nothing about cars), that would restore its performance, maybe even improving it. But I haven't invested in learning about cars because, to be honest, my lack of knowledge about cars doesn't impact me on a day-to-day basis.

But the brain? Well, my brain does impact me. Every minute of every day. So, I have studied it, learned to manage its performance and even improved its performance (even if I do say so myself). And the brain is interesting – scientists are still exploring it and discovering how it works.

I want to give you the tools to RISE; to be **R**esilient and **I**nnovative, to **S**hift and **E**volve, so ensuring your brain can help you navigate and overcome the challenges of work and life. But to do this we need to look under the bonnet to understand the mechanisms of the brain and how to keep it running at peak performance.

1
Brains, Balloons And Biology

The brain works as one system, connecting to different parts depending on what we are doing. In this chapter we'll focus on three parts of the brain that are the most important to understand when learning about how it works. Although each section has a role to play, they all work together.

The limbic system

Collectively, the hypothalamus, basal ganglia, amygdala and hippocampus form part of the brain's limbic system. We can think of this part of the brain as the control room for emotions. This is where emotional responses and the associated hormones are created. This part of the brain works fast. It's almost instantaneous, letting us have immediate emotional responses. It's also partly responsible for memory, which is why we easily remember events that created strong emotions in us.

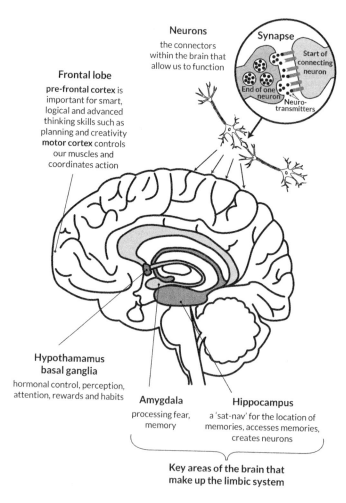

Simplified cross section of the human brain

The frontal lobe

This is the 'clever area' of the brain. It contains a high density of neurons that enable what are referred to as the 'executive functions'. It is responsible for advanced thinking skills: planning, logic, idea creation, decision making, lying (it takes a lot of planning and creativity to lie!), conceptual thinking and rationalisation. In other words, smart thinking.

Neurons

All areas of the brain are connected by pathways, or neurons. They connect thoughts, emotions, actions and behaviours together. The connection point between two neurons is called a synapse; this is where a chemical process takes place to connect the two neurons, or paths, together. Neurons are the paths, while neurotransmitters are the chemical connections between the paths. For example, if you adore Excel spreadsheets and finance, seeing a budget meeting in your diary may excite you because a neuron is connecting thoughts of numbers and formulas with a 'reward' neurotransmitter, like dopamine or glutamate (an excitatory neurotransmitter), giving you positive emotions. If you hate finance, your neurons will connect thoughts of a budget meeting with transmitters that suppress this excitement, giving you negative emotions about the meeting like dread or boredom. The beauty is, you can change how neurons connect, letting you change your thoughts and behaviours. This is called neuroplasticity.

Fight or flight

The purpose of the human brain is to enable our species to survive. It does a pretty good job, given the 7.8 billion humans currently living on the planet.[5] The brain continues to protect us in the same way it has done for the past 20,000 years. It takes in information from our environments, cross-references it with our internal resources and uses these resources to keep us safe by looking out for possible threats. If it sees a threat, the brain knows that it needs to keep you safe by avoiding or moving away from the threat. To do so, it deploys its resources in one of two ways. The first potential response is to fight the threat. If you feel that your boss has made an unfair decision about your pay review, your brain would see that as a threat to your safety, security and perhaps status. You may fight this decision using arguments or resistance (fighting is not just about using your fists). Although technically fighting may involve getting closer to the potential threat, we are essentially trying to remove it by beating it into retreat, so it goes away. These days we tend to 'beat' any threats verbally rather than physically. The second way the brain deals with threats is to take flight. To run away. Again, this does not necessarily mean to physically run away; it might involve avoidance or denial. If you are dreading the budgetary meeting you have scheduled because you are not sure you fully understand the figures, this is a threat to you because you might get found out or ask a stupid question. In response, you decide to take flight: you "suddenly" have another meeting at the same time that you can't miss, or you delegate your attendance to someone else.

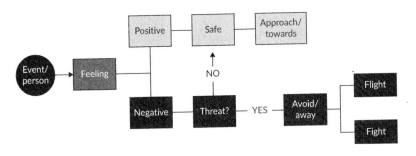

Fight or flight

The term 'fight or flight' is often used along with 'freeze', where you do nothing. The 'freeze' response is usually associated with becoming 'paralysed' with extreme fear. It's not common, thankfully, so in this chapter we will just focus on the 'fight or flight' response to threats.

But first, let's examine what resources are and how the brain uses them.

The brain uses two types of resources to determine whether we are safe. External resources are things outside our head that the brain processes. They include physical sources of information, like your environment and information from others such as the news, emails or data. Physical resources can also include things you need to achieve your goals and tasks: people, money or technology. There are also non-physical sources of information like time, things people say to you and how people treat you.

You also have internal psychological resources that the brain uses: your thoughts, feelings, beliefs, values, attitudes, fears and judgements that happen inside your head. There is lots of research showing that these psychological resources are important for resilience.[6] Experts cite resources ranging from 'authenticity' to 'wisdom' as being key to resilience (sadly I couldn't find any beginning with Z), and not all are easy to change or develop. But in this book, we are looking for more than simple resilience – we are looking for skills and tools to help you RISE.

Think of psychological resources as inputs into our brains. The brain's 100 million neurons are constantly receiving input from both external and internal sources,[7] and we may not be aware of all the input as our brain is able to 'dull' attention paid to non-threatening, regular inputs. You may not be aware of the noise of a plane flying overhead, but if that plane exploded above you the sound would signal a potential threat and focus your attention. Similarly, we are receiving input from within ourselves and often we are unaware of it unless it becomes a problem. We are not aware of how our shoes feel on our feet unless they begin to hurt. We will discuss specific psychological resources in later chapters; for now, consider them 'stuff that goes into your brain' – what you hear, see, touch, taste and smell, as well as thoughts and emotions.

RISE like a hot-air balloon

Despite the obvious jokes about 'air-heads', a hot-air balloon is a great metaphor for the relationship between resources and our brains.

One operates a hot-air balloon by filling it with the right mix of resources (hot and/or cold air, or perhaps propane) so that it strengthens enough to stand upright and then to cut through the surrounding air pressure to rise.

Once in the air, the balloon's pilot constantly monitors the environment using all their senses. The pilot observes what is happening to the balloon, they watch the speed of the clouds and the type of cloud formation. They listen to the air being released from the canisters, the wind, and the creaking of the ropes that wrap around the balloon and the basket. Their sense of smell, and possibly also taste, is on alert for the distinctive metallic-chlorine scent of ozone, which can predict a storm. Most importantly the pilot is tuning in to the rise and fall of the balloon, the strength of wind resistance and any changes in temperature. By evaluating the environment, the pilot can adjust the resource mix accordingly to ensure the balloon remains inflated, stable and afloat, letting its passengers safely reach new heights and gain new perspectives.

It is true that the hot-air balloon is fallible. It operates as a unit: a rip in one part of the balloon may not result in the balloon plunging to the ground but will certainly impact the efficiency of its performance as the resources (in this case, hot air) leak out into the atmosphere. The more rips, the less efficient it is and the more likely it will crash and burn. Steering a hot-air balloon is somewhat hit and miss; you have an idea of where you are going but the Atlantic jet stream may have other ideas. Adjusting the resource mix and the balloon's height may compensate for the jet stream; if not, the resources ensure you get back on the ground safely – wherever that may be. In fact, balloonists see this as part of the fun: you never know where you will end up!

Now, let's compare that with your brain.

We are surrounded by information, some of which can create stress: traffic, family, friends, health, money, whether Newcastle United will make it to the Premier League. To function and 'RISE above' these stresses, your brain needs the right resources. Adding loads of the wrong resources (alcohol, chocolate, binge watching soaps) will not help, nor will an insufficient quantity of the right resource. Trying to inflate a hot-air balloon with a hairdryer – even a three speed one – just won't cut it. A brain that has the right mix of resources will let its owner think clearly, effectively process stimuli from the environment, make better choices, adopt new (and healthier) perspectives and achieve success.

But how do we know what the right resources are? Like the hot-air balloon pilot, we use our senses of sight, sound and smell. But the most powerful way we receive information is through our emotions.

The primary purpose of the brain is to keep us alive. In this respect, little has changed since the evolution of *Homo erectus* 2 million years ago. The brain achieves this objective by differentiating danger from safety using a mechanism that we know as 'feelings'. Feelings are hormonal responses to the environment that tell us whether something is right or wrong, a threat or safe, something to avoid or approach. If we feel lightheaded, nauseous and angry, we probably need food resources. If we have a headache, we may need water. These are, in the simplest terms, the body telling us we are lacking in a resource. Feelings are a complex area that we will explore throughout this book.

As with a hot-air balloon, the input of the right mix of resources into our brains will create SOUND brains, and, like the hot-air balloon, resource-full brains will RISE: be resilient, smart and adaptable. However, it's not about stuffing your head with as many resources as possible; if it was, then this would be a short book. Three factors limit the resources we can give our brains: capacity, load and quality.

Capacity

For a hot-air balloon to carry four passengers, it requires 2.2 million litres of air. For comparison, an Olympic-sized swimming pool holds 2.5 million litres of water. We could try and squeeze in another million litres of air in an attempt to go higher and further for longer, but the balloon has a capacity limit; add more resources than it has capacity for, and it will explode. Like the balloon, there are only so many resources the brain can deal with at once. Too many resources, and the brain will metaphorically explode.

The brain is generally considered to have a finite resource capacity,[8] although this is debated. After all, if you think you have limited resource capacity then you probably will. Those who support the theory of unlimited resources tested whether resources were low by measuring levels of willpower.[9] After all, we all know that when we are tired, hungry or stressed our willpower leaves us and we indulge in cake/chocolate/wine (choose your poison) because our sleep, glucose and cognitive resources are low. Studies found that participants who believed that their resources were limited were more likely to lose willpower. But this might suggest that if you believe you have limited resource capacity, then you will. What the study didn't reveal was whether the belief that one has limited resources was related to how many psychological resources one really had at the time.[10] Perhaps a limited-resource mindset is itself a result of low resource levels, but until there is a definitive answer it is safer to assume that we have a limited resource capacity. This makes our resources precious, things to carefully cultivate and to use wisely. The SOUND individual knows that if something is limited, it is much more valuable, as we saw with toilet roll during the Covid-19 outbreak.

Load

Whether you view resource capacity as limited or unlimited, there is general agreement that facing many demands or stressors depletes your resources.[11] Resilience is having enough resources to meet demand, and when you feel the demands on you are greater than what your resources can handle, then your resilience, or ability to cope, reduces. Imagine a rip in the hot-air balloon. Each rip represents a stressor through which your valuable psychological resources escape. As the balloon incurs more rips, or stressors, it will begin to sink.

Sometimes the overload process is slow, with small rips appearing over time. We have all been there, experiencing stress gradually mounting. A colleague resigns, leaving you with double the work. Your kitchen extension is two months behind schedule, due to the discovery of a rare toad living in your garden, leaving you with a camping stove for an oven and a bucket for a sink. Meanwhile you are worried about child number one, who suddenly spends all his time sitting in his bedroom listening to Pink Floyd / The Smiths / Billie Eilish (select generation-relevant reference). The final straw was the police calling having found your mother wandering around the park in her dressing gown looking for Barry Manilow. Lots of little rips in your balloon, which individually would be manageable but together result in a significant loss of resources.

Sometimes the tear is a huge, unexpected rip that causes a rapid loss of altitude. A big event, such as a bereavement, job loss or illness, enters your life without warning, and all your resources are suddenly consumed by this event, diminishing your ability to deal with other aspects of life.

The technical term for this is 'allostatic load'.[12] 'Allostasis' is the collective term for the brain's adaptation processes that help us manage our resources and maintain equilibrium. When we have to activate resources too often to cope with stressors, the consequence is allostatic load: wear and tear on our resources. This is because, when under stress, we release hormones such as cortisol and adrenaline into our bodies. When we repeatedly deploy these hormones (lots of little rips in the balloon), or deploy them in large amounts (a huge rip), we deprioritise the areas of the brain that control smart thinking and learning.[13] Since cortisol and adrenaline 'eat up' your thinking resources, allostatic load (excessive demand) depletes resources.[14]

Sadly, we don't walk round with indicators of our current resource levels, so when someone lashes out at you for what you consider 'no apparent reason', the reality is that dealing with you required one more resource than they had. The demand on them exceeded their capacity.

What, then, is the resource capacity of a human brain, and what is the minimum number of resources with which we can effectively operate? It depends. For our hot-air balloon, the amount of hot air or propane needed to create and maintain altitude will depend on several factors. The warmer the outside temperature, the more propane or hot air we need. If the balloon is only carrying two passengers rather than ten, we'll need fewer resources. If the balloon already has a few small rips in it, we'll need more air/propane than if there were no rips. Similarly, how you cope with stressors depends on your experience, what else is happening in your environment, your personality and even how your parents dealt with stressors.

The process of allostasis (maintaining equilibrium) is a physiological one involving hormones that control the nervous system, the metabolic system, the gut, the kidneys and the immune system,[15] so your levels of health and fitness can also impact how efficiently you deploy resources to manage stressors.[16] Load is complicated and varies from person to person, day to day. But SOUND people are self-aware enough to know their load limit and manage their resources accordingly.

Quality

Now we know that resources are valuable due to their limited quantity, we need to consider which resources we keep and which we lose. Resources are inputs into our brain, but not all resources are created equally; some add to resource levels and others will deplete our resources, like adding a fox into a henhouse. Since adding any old resource into someone's head will not automatically make them SOUND, quality is an issue.

How do you know which resources to let in? Your brain will send you messages as to which resources to avoid and which to approach – you just need to listen for them. The messages are better known as feelings.

When self-isolating during Covid-19, what made you feel negative and depressed and what improved your mood? Watching horror movies such as *Outbreak*,

Contagion or *I am Legend* might have led to an increase in panic, while watching endless videos of cats on skateboards might have brought you inexplicable joy. The feelings these experiences generated were messages as to whether these inputs were beneficial or not: whether we should approach or avoid the stimuli.

In the context of work, your boss may praise you. That's an input that creates positive 'approach' feelings. Praise and reward are examples of positive resources; they help you RISE. By contrast, being shouted at in front of your colleagues will generate negative 'avoid' feelings; although it's also an input to the brain, it depletes your resources as you have to deploy a whole suite of them to prevent you crying, resigning, shouting back or running away.

Often resources themselves are neither positive nor negative – it is how they are delivered and/or in what context. Getting feedback can be a positive experience in which you learn about yourself, enabling you to RISE. Alternatively, poorly communicated feedback dripping with blame may generate negative feelings, decreasing your ability to RISE. Taking in one negative resource in a sea of positive resources is unlikely to make a significant impact, just as farting into a hot-air balloon (given the 2.2 million litres of much fresher air in there) is unlikely to impact performance. However, if the balloon contained more methane than fresh air, it is likely to lose altitude – and require a can of air freshener!

Good feelings, of course, do not always equal quality resources. Drugs, alcohol, smoking, chocolate, cake, spending sprees and revenge all generate good feelings... initially. The positive feelings generated usually wear off quickly. In small doses, these are fine provided they are not the only positive resources you input. Similarly, quality resources do not always generate good feelings, at first. Running, maths exams and childbirth are tough in the short term but increase resources in the long term. In the case of childbirth, it might be very long term.

There is also the subjective element of quality. Hobfoll defines resources as that which is 'valued by the individual'.[17] What one person values, another may not: some people may see a day spent watching cricket as time well spent, increasing their resources. Not for me, I'm afraid. Spending the day sleeping would be equally, if not more, beneficial for me – and about as exciting.

Ensuring a plentiful supply of resources is a dark art, unique to each individual. While an exact formula will vary from person to person, the overarching principle is: the more positive resources a person has, the greater their ability to cope and manage stressors,[18] and the greater the ability to RISE.

ACTIVITY

Consider the tasks and activities you have done in the last week.

- Which did you enjoy or gain a sense of satisfaction from, or which made you feel energised (even if you were physically tired afterwards)?
- Which of them made you feel negative or grumpy? How much effort did you have to put in to complete a task (how tired did it make you feel)?
- Think of the people around you. Which ones provide you with positive resources, which drain your resources?

Understanding what adds to or depletes our resources will enable us to plan our activities, so the amount of resources going in exceeds those going out. Of course, there are always jobs we have to do that we don't enjoy, but make sure you offset them with positive activities. And, if there are people who create rips in your balloon and deplete your resources, make a choice when (and if) you connect with them.

Key learnings from this chapter

The brain is an interconnected system.

The area of the brain responsible for emotions is fast, so feelings always come first.

You can change how your neurons connect and therefore how your brain works.

Resources are limited, which makes them valuable. Choose your resources wisely.

🎈 The brain responds to a perceived threat by either fighting or running away (fight or flight).

🎈 There are two types of brain resources: positive ones that make us feel good and negative ones that don't.

🎈 For the brain to perform well, it needs more positive resources than negative resources.

2
Resources To RISE

A hot-air balloon filled with the right resources can rise to stratospheric levels. As explained in the previous chapter, our brains filled with the right resources can also RISE. This chapter explains what it means for us to RISE. The brain is constantly evaluating the environment, forming attitudes and beliefs as to whether a situation is safe to approach or whether to avoid it, and the brain conveys these attitudes and beliefs to us through feelings and emotions.

Our initial responses to everything are emotional, and this is because emotional processing is a faster process – eight times faster – than thinking with our 'smart' brain. Emotional processing needs to be so fast because this is what helped us survive in the past.

We needed to instantly decide whether that big kitty with the long teeth was to be approached or avoided. If we had relied on smart but slow thinking to consider our options, perform a risk analysis and create a project plan as to the best way forward, we would have had first-hand experience with those long teeth.

We will address how we deal with and respond to the emotions in Chapters 4–7. For now, just bear in mind that everyone's first response is always emotional. That goes for your friends, colleagues, boss, kids, parents and the bus driver. Whether it's receiving your new timetable, listening to the Premier League draw, a government announcement, a decision to upgrade the IT system at work or even a change in the contents of the vending machine, emotions dictate the first response. None of these events are good or bad in themselves; they just are. It is your emotional response that will evaluate the event (not always correctly) as good (approach) or bad (avoid). The brain treats emotion as a source of information.[19]

Let's say a decision has been made to remove allocated parking spots in the office car park. Each employee has evaluated this information and formed an attitude towards it. Employee A responds angrily to this new parking arrangement. They are losing their allocated space and see it as both a personal slight on their status and as political correctness gone mad.

Employee A's brain has used emotion as information. Their negative emotional response has resulted in a negative resource. This type of information processing is termed 'peripheral processing'.[20] Emotionally driven, it requires few resources because it relies on past information and experience, so we don't have to process, evaluate or think too much.[21] One of the reasons we are greater risk takers when we are younger is that we have less knowledge or experience to inform our decisions. When I consider the gap year I spent throwing myself out of airplanes and off bridges tied to a piece of elastic, I wonder what possessed me. Happily for me at the time, what I didn't possess was any knowledge or experience about how either activity could go wrong.

Luckily, if we have sufficient resources, we can also apply conscious thought to situations when appropriate. Employee B also had an immediate negative emotional response to the change in parking arrangements and wonders if sometimes the organisation makes changes for change's sake. However, Employee B has since thought about it and is now feeling more positive. They can see it is probably fairer and, after all, more people are working from home now.

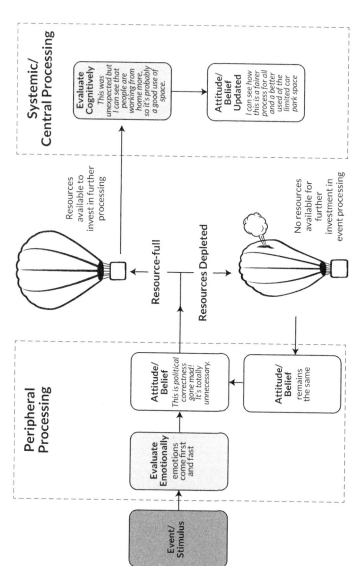

Systemic/Central Processing

Evaluate Cognitively
This was unexpected but I can see that people are working from home more, so it's probably a good use of space.

Attitude/Belief Updated
I can see how this is a fairer process for all and a better used of the limited car park space

Resources available to invest in further processing

Resource-full

Resources Depleted

No resources available for further investment in event processing

Peripheral Processing

Attitude/Belief
This is political correctness gone mad! It's totally unnecessary.

Attitude/Belief remains the same

Evaluate Emotionally
emotions come first and fast

Event/Stimulus

Emotional and cognitive evaluations

Employee B's additional thinking time generates a positive input into their brain and therefore adds to their resource level. Referred to as systemic or central processing, this requires investing some resources into cognitive processing and reflection.[22] Employee A's instant, emotional reaction to the new parking system was negative. However, if Employee A applies some thought, they may realise that this was not a policy designed to personally annoy them and that it's probably a more efficient use of limited parking spaces. This thought process mediates the initial emotion (anger)[23] and the negative resource becomes at least neutral, if not positive.

This cognitive processing and reflection is only possible if Employee A has the resources available to invest in further thinking beyond an emotional response. Research has shown that where resources are lacking, evaluations of the environment and events remain emotional.[24]

The output of evaluative processes are attitudes and beliefs. We are more likely to create positive attitudes when resources are plentiful because plentiful resources enable investment in logical thinking; otherwise, we rely only on our 'first and fast' emotional responses, which create bias and prejudice. I have yet to determine what event or stimulus created my prejudice against men wearing soccer shirts (outside of a soccer match), but in being aware of the attitude I can invest resources in changing this illogical bias.

I still *feel* the emotion, but I have the resources to manage it and tell myself to think differently. Eventually, my brain will be reprogrammed when seeing a man in a soccer shirt from thinking: 'There's a man looking for a fight' to thinking 'There's a man who enjoys watching sport and is proud of his team'.

People with fewer psychological resources will be less able to see events as positive, and this adds negative resources to their balloon, making it sink and reducing their resilience. Being able to apply systemic or central processing to the environment or events is key to being able to RISE. Choosing to evaluate the things around us positively (or reframe them, if required) adds to our resources and helps create resilience: the first component of RISE.

R is for resilience

The definition of resilience is hard to pin down.[25] Most definitions of resilience refer to maintaining equilibrium or returning to normal functioning after a challenge.[26] Resilience is the result of our normal adaptation systems – the process of allostasis.[27] It's maintaining your resources to allow you to manage life: keeping the balloon afloat.

Some definitions broaden the idea of resilience, believing it's not only about maintaining equilibrium but also includes the process of bouncing back from adversity.[28] In other words, re-floating the balloon after events have caused it to sink to the ground.

There are some that go even further, asserting that resilience is not just about surviving adversity and bouncing back but also about thriving, learning and growing as a result of the adversity.[29] There is research both for[30] and against this thinking.[31]

There are a couple of issues with the latter conception of resilience. Firstly, what is meant by thriving and growth? Studies differ in their measurement: some include behaviours such as stopping drinking,[32] adopting deeper religious beliefs,[33] not taking life for granted,[34] and psychological changes such as having a sense of personal strength and increased spirituality.[35] Furthermore, if growth was an inevitable part of resilience, every person who demonstrated resilience would grow from their challenging experience, which sadly is not always the case.[36] In an eighteen-year study of resilience in disadvantaged children, Egeland, Carlson and Sroufe found that adverse situations had a cumulative negative effect on ability rather than providing opportunities for growth beyond equilibrium.[37] The few who successfully 'bounced back' achieved what society would consider 'normal functioning'. Given the background of the participants, was this evidence of growth or merely reaching what society considers an acceptable level of equilibrium and functioning? It's also worth noting that if bouncing back is required, then the deployment of resources has already failed. Had the individual been able to maintain resilience, they would have nothing from which to bounce back in the first place.

Where the confusion lies is in combining two different motivational mechanisms and labelling them both 'resilience'. The first is our defensive motivational system: the drive to protect ourselves against harm, whether physical, emotional or financial. Often triggered by an emotional event, the defensive motivational system deploys resources to help us maintain equilibrium.[38] Using our hot-air balloon analogy, we are floating along, with adequate resources enabling us to maintain altitude and head in the right direction, when along comes an unexpected gust of wind that unsteadies the balloon, causing it to lose height and change direction. The pilot will use all the resources at their disposal to return the balloon to its original position, but what if there are no more resources? The air tanks are empty, the pilot has run out of ideas and the balloon has insufficient resources to counteract the demands of the weather; thus, the balloon heads towards earth. At this stage, the motivation for using our resources is focused on defensive activities: preventing harm in the form of a sudden and rapid impact with the ground. During this time, emotions are probably running high, and if these emotions are negative (most likely in the face of impending doom), research has shown that the ability to utilise systemic or central processing to apply reasoned and logical thinking is inhibited.[39] Whether the balloon actually hits the ground will depend on something changing: finding more resources or the weather changing.

Now, imagine if during the middle of this crisis, while you are trying to avoid death by balloon, you are asked to learn or do something you have never done before. While all your resources are focused on staying alive (defensive motivation), your boss is asking you to listen to them and absorb the new procedure for raising purchase orders. What is the likelihood you will be listening intently and learning? As listening and learning require using your smart brain (systemic or central processing), I would say the likelihood is slim to non-existent. Your balloon resources are depleted and you're spending the few resources you have on preventing an impending collision. The defensive motivational system uses what few resources we have to do exactly that: defend.

Learning and growing comes from a different type of motivation: the appetite motivational system. Thriving and growing require us to learn new things, to reflect and to create new neuronal connections; therefore, we can only activate it when there is a plentiful supply of resources and when we feel safe.[40] When we have the time and the resources to move from the quick, instinctive emotional responses of our defensive motivational system to the relative calm of the considered thoughts of our central processing system, we have the capacity to learn.

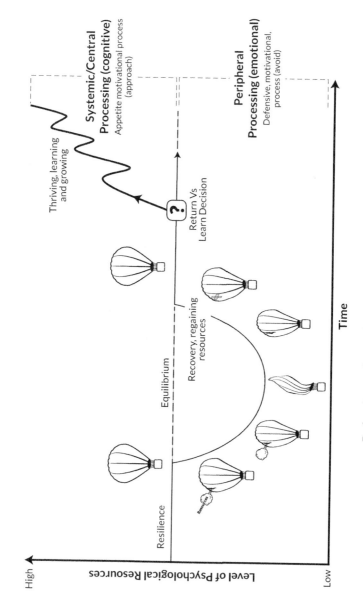

Defensive and appetite motivational processes

Level of Psychological Resources

High

Low

Time

Resilience

Equilibrium

Recovery, regaining resources

Return Vs Learn Decision

Thriving, learning and growing

Systemic/Central Processing (cognitive)
Appetite motivational process (approach)

Peripheral Processing (emotional)
Defensive, motivational, process (avoid)

Not everyone grows and learns from adversity; some people merely return to previous levels of equilibrium. There are many reasons for this, which we will discuss in the next chapter, but this is a choice and it leads to a 'return vs learn' decision. At this point, do you breathe a sigh of relief and continue along your merry way, or do you take time to reflect and learn from the process?

After examining the defensive and appetite motivational processes, it seems resilience, recovery and growth are also separate processes.[41] Resilience is the ability to continually deploy resources to maintain equilibrium.[42] Recovery is the process of replenishing your resources to return to equilibrium, and it is only at the recovery point that you will have resources available to learn and grow. What researchers do agree on is that having enough of the right psychological resources enables resilience.[43]

Those who are SOUND are resilient because they know how to maintain the resources that they have or create new ones if needed. If there is a 'dip' in their resilience, they are able to recover from it more quickly than someone who is not SOUND. In being resilient, they also have sufficient resources for initiative.

I is for initiative

Initiative is defined by Fay and Frese (2001) as, among other things, the capacity to think independently, be inventive, cope with setbacks proactively and with persistence. These days, we need to be able to use our initiative more than ever because new and unexpected challenges ('unknown unknowns'[44]) are popping up with increasing frequency. Just look at Covid-19 – it was something that no one had come across before. Although some people had prior experiences to draw on, such as those who had lived through epidemics, this was a new problem that required a new solution. Technology drives constant change in the world, presenting us with new situations or questions with no right or wrong answer. We need to recognise problems and be bold in developing innovative ways to solve them. SOUND people are able to do this because they are resource-full. They have the resources to invest in the smart thinking needed for initiative.

If we are investing our resources just trying to stay afloat (in equilibrium), or we're trying to replenish our resources to return to equilibrium, we do not have the resource capacity to invest in smart and creative thinking, and we are less likely to be able to apply initiative.

In our balloon scenario, when the bad weather hits, the pilot's attention is focused, and like a well-oiled machine the pilot manages the balloon by adjusting its resources. Any resource not needed to keep that balloon in the air is dispensed with; picnic baskets, cameras, binoculars and bottles of champagne all go overboard. They are not key resources for keeping afloat. No, not even the champagne.

The same happens to us internally. When we get a rip in our balloon and feel negative emotions as a result of danger or a threat, the brain responds by increasing our cortisol and adrenaline. These are not 'bad' hormones as they enable speedy (and thus lifesaving) responses by strengthening the neurons that connect the areas of the brain that are responsible for memory retrieval (hippocampus) and smart thinking (pre-frontal cortex). This enables you to respond based on either experience (memories) or by making a plan (smart thinking). This is a clever survival mechanism, but it only works to a point.

If a balloon hits a force 10 storm, suffering multiple rips or a huge tear, the resource loss can be severe. A similarly dangerous or threatening experience in your life can cause so much stress you don't feel you have sufficient resources to cope, at which point cortisol and adrenaline increase even further. This increase now disables the link between the clever prefrontal cortex and the memory-retrieving hippocampus. You can no longer remember things or come up with a plan.

These hormones go so far as to shut off some of your bodily functions and mental resources. Specifically, they disable the ones you don't need for fight or flight, just as the balloon pilot got rid of anything that did not help it float. Cortisol and adrenaline may disrupt your digestive process (so you might feel sick or have 'butterflies' in your tummy). The increase in adrenaline may make you want to pee often because the adrenal glands sit above the kidneys. Your heart rate may increase, getting you ready to run or fight, which in turn increases your temperature (sweating). Your peripheral vision narrows[45] and your hearing also reduces,[46] helping you to react quickly by forcing you to focus on only the information needed to survive.

The cost of this quicker response and survival mechanism is that resources in the 'smart' part of your brain are shut down: just like the picnic basket and champagne in the balloon, these are thrown overboard during a crisis. Fighting or running away doesn't require knowledge of Greek mythology, quadratic equations, or the company's debt to equity ratio for the last four years.

Have you ever had a big argument with someone and it was only afterwards you thought of something clever you should have said? During the argument, the part of your brain responsible for witty put-downs was probably 'offline' as your brain was in 'fight' mode. When operating in this survival mode, your reduced resources result in a narrower view since you don't have the resources to process anything beyond your emotions and the here and now. It's not that you are not capable of thought and consideration; rather, at that point in time, you didn't have access to the cognitive resources needed to be smart or show initiative.

If some stress can help thinking but too much stress reduces our ability to think, to show initiative you need to be in an emotional state that enables smart thinking. That means low cortisol/adrenaline and high dopamine.

Dopamine neurons enable the parts of the brain responsible for learning, recalling memories and thinking creatively to work efficiently.[47] They are also associated with feeling happy and with positive mood.[48] When cortisol is high, dopamine is reduced. When dopamine is high, cortisol is reduced. So, how do you activate your dopamine neurons?[49] By having enough positive psychological resources to keep your balloon riding high. When you feel happy, safe and threat-free, your dopamine is high and you activate the smart part of your brain, allowing you to think, be smart and take a logical view of emotions (process them using systematic processing). The frontal cortex of the brain manages the balance, if it has sufficient resources!

Having sufficient resources to think beyond the initial emotional responses to more thought-through responses allows further processing. As a result, you're able to see the bigger picture[50] – like Employee B, who was able to think beyond themselves to understand the context and reason behind the decision to change the parking arrangements.

Having plentiful resources enables activation of the smart part of our brain. It even allows us to invest resources into creative and innovative ideas, knowing that the investment may not pay off. Not all creative ideas work, after all. One creative individual thought of (and manufactured) a boiled egg squarer, which makes your hard-boiled eggs square. Including the yolk. It never took off (can't think why), but it shows that at some point someone had enough surplus resources to invest in creating something new. OK, this one wasn't particularly successful, but it only takes one working idea...

S is for shifting

Up to this point we have seen that there are two approaches to interpreting the world: emotional and cognitive. These approaches are also known as 'heart vs head', 'System 1 and System 2' or 'fast and slow thinking'.[51] Both approaches have their pros and cons, and it is the tension between these that often makes decisions difficult.

Often, the head tells us we need to do something but the heart feels heavy because we don't want to do it. You know that starting to file the stack of papers marked 'For Filing' that has been piling up for the last six months is the right thing to do (head), but you would rather be redesigning the new poster for the Christmas party (heart). Sometimes the head wins, sometimes the heart. The key is being able to shift between these perspectives to ensure you are evaluating all the information: the logical and practical versus the emotional and wishful. And if you can shift between these perspectives, you can shift between other perspectives. Which is useful because everything has an alternative perspective. You don't have to agree with another perspective, but being able to see where other people are coming from enables smart thinking, creative thinking, compassion and tolerance.

Low level of resources: emotional responses	High level of resources: emotional & cognitive responses
Narrow focus, what's in it for me	AND big picture, what's in it for others
The here and now	AND the future
Exploit	AND explore

A crucial part of being able to manage change, either in or outside of work, is the ability to shift between the exploit and explore perspectives. Deciding whether to exploit existing resources or to explore new ones is a survival decision. Consider the great Serengeti migration of wildebeest: from January to March, the herd are to be found in the south of the Serengeti feeding on the short grass and drinking from waterholes that were replenished during the rains of December. The herd is exploiting the favourable environment to feed and calve. However, by March the grass is eroded, the watering holes drying up. The herd could stay where they are, eking out an existence by exploiting the little remaining grass and water, but there is a risk here. There may not be enough food or water to go around and herd members may die of starvation. They decide to move, exploring alternative food sources, although this, too, is risky. They may not find a new grassy nirvana, and herd members may (and do) die during such a treacherous journey, but they know that staying where they are will lead to certain starvation.

Exploring is scary. It's the unknown. There might be nothing out there, or there is something but you don't know how to deal with it. It's safer to stay where you are, exploiting what you have, in an environment you are familiar with.

Spencer Johnson's book *Who Moved My Cheese*[52] explains this survival decisions pattern in the context of organisational change in an easy-to-read way. In days gone by, organisations were filled with people who did the same job, in the same place with the same people for many years – sometimes their whole working lives. It was safe. The employee knew what they were doing; risk was minimal. Why on earth would they risk exploring something new?

To answer this question, let's consider the example of changing jobs and workplaces. If you've ever taken on a new job in a new company, what were your reasons for deciding to stop exploiting what you knew and explore something different? Often, there is more than one reason, but your motivations will be either to avoid (I hate my boss and need to get away from them) or to approach (I want to get experience in a new sector) or some of both.

In today's organisations, change and its increasing pace have become the norm.[53] The consequence of such rapid and continuous change is that organisations are less predictable and stable,[54] resulting in increased ambiguity and uncertainty.[55] It's all scary, now. We are expected to be able to cleverly exploit what we have available, while also exploring innovative ways to do things.

Some people have a preference for exploiting: if they were a wildebeest, they would rather manage on the meagre pickings of a dry savannah than risk leaving what they know for the potential of new feeding grounds. The advantage of this is a level of certainty and comfort: they know what they are getting, they are familiar with their surroundings and, despite the difficulties, they have learned to manage.

Other people are explore-orientated, always looking for something new. As wildebeests, they would
have set out for new pastures long before the drought
set in, usually because they were bored with the current grass. This can also be risky because not only
might they find no new grass, they could be left on
their own and vulnerable.

While there are pros and cons to both approaches,
change requires the ability to flex between explore
and exploit. As the table above shows, however, you
can only flex if you have enough cognitive resources
to do so.

When resources are low, our focus narrows to the
immediate and personal, such as 'What does the
change mean for me and my job?' Exploring a new
situation or opportunity may mean learning and
doing something different, and you may not have the
resources for that if you are investing them into survival. Furthermore, the pressure to change is causing
more rips in your balloon, resulting in the loss of more
resources as you are pushed more into survival mode
and away from smart thinking. The downward spiral
continues and, if unchecked, it can lead to stress and
mental health issues.

Those who are resource-full are able to move beyond
the 'What does that mean for me?' emotional
response to see the bigger picture beyond themselves: their team, the organisation, the customer or

the strategy. They can shift from explore to exploit, seeing both the now and the future. When finding solutions, they are able to exploit the known and existing solutions and to explore untried innovative options, combining the best of both if needed. When making decisions, they can evaluate what is best for the organisation and the employees, now and in the future. They are able to flex and broaden their thinking and responses, resulting in better decision making and problem solving.

A further benefit of being willing and able to explore is the ability to grow and learn. Those who sit happily in the same job for ten years have one year's experience repeated ten times over, rather than ten years' cumulative experience, so we need to be able to explore to be able to evolve.

E is for evolving

Being able to shift thinking is key to evolving. After all, if the wildebeests weren't able to take the explore option, they would have died out by now. As Darwin noted, it is those who are able to evolve that survive. And just as organisations need to evolve to survive, so do the employees within them.

As well as evolving out of necessity, SOUND people evolve by choice. They see themselves as works in progress, learning and growing with each passing

RISE

year. They evolve not just because another person or an organisation requires them to, but because they want to. They are exploring who they are, unafraid of new experiences and alternative viewpoints. Returning to equilibrium is not an option for them; at the point of the 'return or learn' decision, they choose to learn and grow from adversity.

Evolving is not surface-level learning based on your defence motivation system; it is deeper self-learning from your appetite motivation system. Let's say you are working on a team project and realise there is an error in the work you have submitted. You can fix it, but it will take time – time you don't have because the deadline is tomorrow. Rather than cover up the error, you decide to come clean with your boss, who responds angrily and demands that you fix the error but won't extend your deadline.

What's the learning here?

We all respond emotionally at first, showing surface-level learning using peripheral processing, coming from a defensive motivation. Your 'avoid' learnings may be that your boss hates bad news or is emotionally volatile and that you should 'never admit your mistakes – next time, cover them up'. You return to the task and carry on as before, but your resources are now deployed in ensuring your error is not discovered.

If you are resource-full, on the other hand, you can invest your resources in gaining deeper learnings using your appetite motivation (approach/toward). To enable evolutionary learning, consider asking yourself:

- Why did I make that mistake? What do I need to do differently in future?
- How might I have approached my boss differently to get a different response?

In this example, it's true your boss could have responded differently, but we are all human and your boss may have been having a bad day. After they have calmed down, they may decide to sit with you to ask the questions that create deeper learning. Or not. It doesn't matter, because if you are SOUND you will ask these questions of yourself since they promote learning through self-exploration and understanding. This adds to your resources.

Evolving does not create immunity from resource loss. If we zoom in on the 'thriving, learning and growing' line in our model earlier in the chapter, we can see that although the trend is upward, there are moments when our resources deplete because learning about ourselves can be challenging. To learn, we need to make mistakes and then get feedback. This can be unpleasant because it involves recognising where there is a gap in our skills, knowledge or behaviour.

For many years, I worked in a financial services company managing a team of around thirty people. I threw myself into my job – at my desk by 7am, not leaving until after 6pm. Our department was achieving great success: measures were in place and customers were happy. If only the team was a bit more enthusiastic. After about six months, I received some feedback from HR that my team was not happy. How could this be? We had transformed and we were successful; surely I was an amazing boss. Apparently not.

Although it was never explicitly stated, the team felt that they were expected to work the same long hours I did, my behaviour implicitly communicating this. I was the first in and the last out. As far as the team were concerned, I was always at work and that was the standard I set – a standard they felt they were failing to meet. If you think you are failing, then your resources will deplete. I had a team with low resources for this reason, and I'd been wondering why they weren't enthusiastic about the changes in the department.

I was shocked. It was never my intention to make my team feel like failures! I began unpicking my actions, recognising how my behaviour as a leader set the 'rules', intentionally or otherwise. This led to many soul-searching questions about why I behave the way I do, my drivers and who I was. There were some uncomfortable answers, which tested my resilience, and I questioned myself as a leader. Because of this learning, I evolved as a person and a leader and continued to thrive and grow. Evolutionary learning consumes resources, which means you can only learn if you have the resources available to invest in the quest for learning.

Learning is a biological process in the brain. It involves the creation of neurons that connect together. It is hugely complex and there is still much to learn about the brain, but for the sake of understanding the process of learning, here is a simplified description.

Imagine a person who has developed a phobia of dogs after being bitten by one when they were ten years old. The phobia is caused by a memory that was created when a neuron connected 'dog' with 'bite'. Without intervention, every time the child sees a dog the neuron between 'dog' and 'bite' gets stronger, reinforcing the association. To protect against any future pain from dog bites, the brain creates an emotional response to send a message of 'avoid'. In this case, the emotion is fear. This is a learned response.

The stimulus itself is neither good nor bad, neither positive nor negative; it is how we interpret it and what we associate it with that creates this judgement. This relates to our learned responses since learning is about creating new neurons with new connections. Sometimes we have to 'unlearn' as well – if we change the way we do something, we need to unlearn the old way and learn the new one. This means 'rewiring' the neuron. The more we use the new neuron, the stronger the connection gets; the less we use a neuron, the weaker it gets. This explains why if you don't practise and continually use a neuronal connection, it will fade.

For a dog phobia, new learning needs to take place to change the response to the 'dog' stimulus.

This takes effort. Just think of when you have tried to change the way you do something: give up smoking, stop using the word 'but', start exercising more. We use a lot of brain energy stopping the habit, unlearning it and trying to rewire the neuron. It takes great effort, and when we are low on resources the effort may be too great because we need our resources to survive, not improve.

The key to strengthening the efficiency of neurons is dopamine. The neurotransmitter that depletes with cortisol. This is why making a change is often too strenuous for us when we are low on resources. Just think of how difficult it is to exercise willpower when you are tired, hungry or thirsty.

Having a resource-full brain will help us RISE – be Resilient, use our Initiative, Shift our thinking and Evolve. In Chapter 4, we will look at which resources make us SOUND and help us RISE. But first, in Chapter 3, we'll learn about the thing that causes the most loss of resources: fear.

ACTIVITY

Recall an event from last week. Chances are, the event you recall prompted an emotional response, and I bet it was a negative one. This is because the amygdala and hippocampus, the parts of the brain that create negative emotional responses, also have a role to play in memory. That's why we can more easily remember bad things: it's a survival mechanism to tell us not to put ourselves in that position again.

As you recall the emotional response you had:

- Describe the emotion to yourself.
- Was it a towards/approach emotion or an away/ avoid emotion?
- What did you do with the emotion? Did you accept it and carry it around, or did you change it? If you managed to change it, how?

Here's an example:

Last week, I got angry with my neighbour because they were making a noise in their front garden while I was trying to have an afternoon nap. I was grumpy because I was tired, but I was also annoyed because I wasn't able to do what I wanted (sleep) due to their noisy gardening.

The desire to sleep was a 'toward' emotion: I wanted to rest and feel better. I was angry because their noise was preventing my blissful siesta. Rather than leaning out of the window and yelling at my neighbour, which was my first response and a result of peripheral processing, I did nothing about the noise. Through systemic processing

I realised that it was unreasonable to expect people to be quiet at 2pm, so I couldn't complain. I decided to get an early night instead.

Key learnings from this chapter

- Emotions always come first and fast.

- Emotions or feelings are messages from your brain.

- When cortisol and adrenaline are high, we feel stressed. When dopamine is high, we feel happy. We can't have both.

- We need many brain resources to learn, grow, shift our thinking and be resilient.

- We are motivated into action because we are either avoiding something or approaching something. Avoiding causes stress, adrenaline and cortisol. Approaching results in rewards, feeling good and dopamine.

3
The Rock Of Fear

By this point I would like to think the science has convinced you that it's better to have more positive psychological resources in the brain than negative ones – in other words, to be SOUND – but there is one thing that will eat up your positive resources quicker than a cough can clear a pub: fear.

Fear is not a bad thing per se. It is a valuable warning signal, albeit a powerful one, but it needs to be to ensure our survival. Imagine if we could turn off our fear. The number of dumb things I would do, I am not sure I would last a day. I certainly would not have made it through my gap year. However, fear triggers our defensive mechanisms: cortisol and 'avoid' responses. It narrows our focus, prioritising only the resources we need to survive. Fear doesn't have to be logical, as my fear of cruise ships attests (I've never even been on a cruise ship!). Fear is so powerful it can defy logic.

Imagine I lay a plank of wood 3 metres long and half a metre wide on the ground (that's about 10ft by 1.5ft in old money). If I bet you your tipple of choice that you couldn't walk along it, you would likely accept the bet and win the drink. No problem.

Now, if I were to place the same plank between the roofs of two ten-storey buildings, would you still take the bet? You know you can walk the plank, so logically you can take on the bet, but fear has kicked in. Maybe if I offered you a larger incentive you'd take the bet; however, the incentive would vary for different people. It would depend on the tension between your defensive motivation (the value of protecting what you have, namely your life) and your appetite motivation (the value of what you may gain).

Going back to our balloon metaphor, we all drag our fears with us like a rock. The Rock of Fear (in my head this is said in a booming, ominous voice, maybe with a spooky soundtrack) is the weight of our fears we carry with us. This is why you can't run away from your fears; whichever direction the balloon of life takes you, your fears are right there with you. So, for our balloon to RISE we need sufficient resources to elevate the balloon *and* the Rock of Fear. If your fear is boulder sized, you will need a large number of resources to maintain equilibrium and RISE, and you'll find this difficult and exhausting. A small rip in the balloon will have a greater effect on your equilibrium than it would for someone with only a pebble of fear. A pebble of fear will also weigh you down but won't consume as many resources; thus, replenishment of resources will be easier, enabling a quicker return to equilibrium.

There are many names for fear that manifest in behaviour. Anger is a common one. Anger is the only emotion that is both approach and avoid. Combined with sufficient resources, the appetite motivational system can use anger constructively to change things for the better. The women's suffrage movement, unions and the anti-apartheid movement, among many other initiatives, were all born out of anger at injustice. However, without sufficient resources, the defensive motivational system will drive our anger, resulting in behaviours such as avoiding people, situations or change.

Other emotions with fear at their core include guilt, embarrassment, sadness, panic, grief, regret, defeat, resentment, failure and shame. There are few people who will say, 'I am unhappy about this because I fear I am not good enough' or 'I don't want to fail'. You are more likely to hear people say things like, 'Nah, I don't want to do it' or 'It's stupid' or maybe 'I don't see why I have to do it'. The latter are all 'avoid' strategies. Think of when you have decided not to do something such as play a sport, take on a new job, create something, present to a large audience or learn a new topic – why did you decline to do it? Be honest, now.

A note on **anxiety** and **depression:**

These are clinical conditions in which, to continue with our metaphor, the Rock of Fear has become so big that it disables the individual's normal functioning. The fear 'eats' resources, becoming larger and requiring ever more resources to feed on as it grows. This downward spiral **requires professional support**. This book is not designed for those who need this type of mental health support.

If you feel overwhelmed or depressed or have thoughts of self-harm, put down this book and seek help **now**. Speak to someone: your partner, a colleague, a friend or your doctor. Alternatively, seek out organisations that provide this type of professional help in your area.

The 5 Cs of comfort

Understanding fear is a personal journey, digging beneath the surface to examine the source of fear. Some people live their whole lives and have no idea where their fears come from. They don't understand themselves and their motivations and so miss out on some great opportunities in life because of fear.

Luckily, humans have some common, inherent fears that have enabled the survival of the species, and they provide a good place to start in analysing our own fears. These common fears have been 'programmed' into the human brain, and we pass on these effective protection mechanisms from generation to generation. We have the same fears we had when we were cave dwellers, and they haven't changed much because these fears have proved so successful in helping the human species survive.

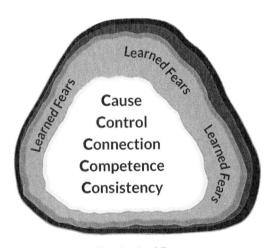

The Rock of Fear

If we could look inside the Rock of Fear, we would see that our core fears fall into five categories, all of which stem from the drive to survive. These categories are the 5 Cs of comfort.

Cause: 'What's the point?'

We need to know why we do the things we do. We have a limited number of resources – what are we investing them in? A cause provides meaning and purpose. Our cave-dwelling ancestors invested resources in creating tools to feed and defend their families. There was reward for these efforts: a healthy tribe. Conversely, to perform an action without a known cause risks loss of time and resources. When we're at work, not only do we need to know why we are performing each task, we also need to understand why we are working in the first place. What is our purpose?

Control: 'Am I in control?'

Ever wondered why people hate being told what to do? It's natural that we all like to have control over our own actions or decisions; after all, putting them in the hands of someone else is a risk. Having a sense of control provides security, and being the master of your own destiny provides a sense of safety.

Connectedness: 'Am I likeable?'

Humans are pack animals. There is safety in numbers. To be thrown out of our cave-community was risky for our ancestors: survival alone was unlikely. We need to feel part of a unit, which is why we create in-groups and out-groups. You are either in my tribe (safe) or another tribe (a threat). We still have tribes today: football clubs, political parties, music fan groups and the like. These groups are part of who we are and the sense of belonging they create is particularly important in young adulthood.

Competence: 'Am I good enough?'

Are we capable of dealing with what life throws at us? If we face a challenge that we don't think we have the skills to address, the brain sees that challenge as a threat. Early humans who did not master the art of hunting would starve, so we learned that being competent increases our chances of survival. In today's workplaces, where we are defined by how good we are at our jobs, and rewarded or punished according to our performance, lacking competence can have far-reaching consequences. We therefore need to be seen as capable and competent, and some people will go to great lengths to create this impression.

Consistency: 'Is this familiar?'

When we face a situation that's new or out of the ordinary, from a survival perspective the smart thing to do is to assume the new element is a threat – otherwise, the first time our ancestors stumbled across the kitty with the big teeth would have been the last. This is why whenever something unexpected happens, our brain will assume it is a threat. Imagine at 5pm on a

Friday your boss says, 'I need to see you first thing Monday morning'. If this is not a scheduled meeting, your first emotional response will be: 'Uh oh, this is unusual… What have I done?' You will then spend the weekend worrying about it.

As if these '5 C' fears weren't enough, as we move through life we accumulate more 'learned' fears. A bad experience at the dentist, being thrown in the swimming pool when you can't swim, the pain of an injection or being laughed at on the playground can all create emotional 'avoid' memories.

Not all fears are created equal, and they change in priority depending on what is important to us. For young children, consistency is critical to feeling safe. As we grow, control becomes important: children begin to realise that they are independent from their parents and want to make decisions for themselves, leading to tantrums when they want to go to school in nothing but their underpants but Mum is having none of it. Connection with peers becomes critical as we approach young adulthood because we are finding our own identities and we want to be accepted and liked. Later in life, we may not give a stuff what other people think; we are more focused on competence and cause.

The size of each fear depends on many things: experience, how we've been brought up, what we have been told as a child, our personality and the culture in which we were raised. I was brought up by strict parents – the type who think children should be seen and not heard. My sister and I usually did what we were told or there would be hell to pay. No arguments, no discussion: just obey.

Now, decades later, lack of control is probably my biggest fear. I don't want to go back to being told what to do, and whenever something happens that I can't control my fear wakes up and I feel stressed. This increases cortisol and adrenaline, and the smart part of my brain is overruled by my limbic system. If unchecked, I act emotionally. My boss almost found this out when she gave me a task and told me, 'Don't ask questions, just do it'. I was furious. My fear had not only woken up but risen up to Hulk size, ripping my balloon. I stomped away, sat at my desk and seethed. How dare my boss speak to me like that! She had no right.

I look back now and think about how I might have spoken to my boss the next time I saw her, given the negative feelings I had about her at that time. I might have done something I would regret, something which I would have to apologise for later.

Luckily, my brain had a surplus of resources that enabled me to apply some logical thinking to the event. My boss didn't normally speak to me like that, so I decided she must have had good reason. I was able to go back to her calmly and ask if everything was OK, because I was surprised at the way she spoke to me. It turns out, she was unable to tell me the reason for giving me the task due to its confidentiality, and she was under a huge amount of pressure. She ended up apologising to me for not being more sensitive.

Did I get information as to why I needed to do the task? No, it was still confidential. Life is not Disney, and not every story has a happy ending. But, in having the resources to process the information using the smart part of my brain – to look at the big picture, see alternative views and recognise that it was my fears that had created my emotions – I was able to deal with the situation in a positive way. This reflects research that shows those with greater resources are better able to process potentially negative facts in a systemic way, creating a more positive attitude at best and an acceptance of the situation at worst.[56]

We all have fears; it's normal. In the remaining chapters I will highlight underlying fears by writing them in **bold font**. The fears we feel are not always obvious. We become masters of hiding and suppressing fears and thus learn to function despite them. This is because surrounding our Rock of Fear is an army: our Ego Army.

The Ego Army

A person's Rock of Fear is a bit like their genitals. We all have them, but we only show them to a select few.

Just as we cover our nakedness with clothes, we each spend a lot of time, effort and resources covering our Rock of Fear using a wrapping called 'ego'.

The purpose of the ego wrapping is the same for all: to protect us. It is the nature of the wrapping that will influence how we interact with the outside world.

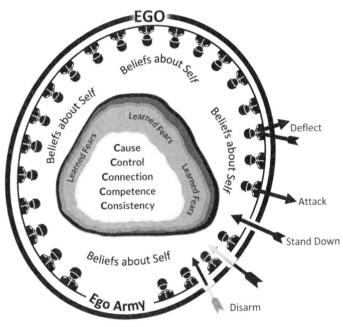

The Ego Army and our Rock of Fear

Consider your ego as an army, a line of soldiers protecting you from anything that might stimulate a fear or shake your self-belief. Your fears or self-belief could be unfounded, but the army doesn't care. They are trained to protect the Rock of Fear and associated self-beliefs, and they will respond immediately by deflecting, attacking, standing down or disarming any inputs.

Some say that attack is the best form of defence. When our army senses our fears awakening, it attempts to prevent this, and the associated pain, by attacking. We can see this in arguments when people say, 'Well, it was your fault because you did X'. It's also a common approach for political parties: attack the opponents, and hopefully the people won't notice our deficiencies.

The Ego Army does let some stimuli through. Anything that is positive and will support our self-beliefs (whether they are right or wrong) will get a free pass. Sometimes this means disarming comments so that they align with our self-beliefs. Misalignment between what we see or hear and our self-perception can cause emotional pain (and use up resources). The Ego Army might disarm negative comments, turning them into less negative ones by taking the 'ammunition' out of them. The army may respond to negative comments by adding thoughts like 'They are jealous of my success' or 'I am just too intelligent for them' or 'They are idiots'.

Similarly, the Ego Army may disarm positive comments, turning them into negative ones because a negative version of the comment aligns with our self-belief. The Ego Army may disarm a compliment like 'Good job' by thinking, 'It was luck, not skill'.

Not everyone trains and deploys their army in the same way. Our armies receive their orders from our neurons, which have taught them when to attack and when to stand down based on our experiences and beliefs about ourselves. As a result of living in a 'shouty' family, and despite strict parents, I learned that when shouted at, you shout back. My neurons provided my army with this order, which it carried out in exemplary fashion. However, when I entered the workplace, it turned out that this was not an effective strategy for maintaining a job. I needed to change the order to my army. How did I do this? In the second part of the book, we will look at ways to do this but, for now, know that how the army responds is up to you.

Everyone has a choice regarding the extent to which the Ego Army protects our fears and determines our behaviour. SOUND individuals are aware of their fears. By understanding them, they begin to chip away at their Rock of Fear and better manage their army. There are two strategies to enable you to RISE despite your fears: constantly fill the balloon with the right resources or reduce the size of the Rock of Fear. Preferably, you will use both.

ACTIVITY

- Recall an experience that generated an emotional response. Why did you have the response? Which fear was being activated?

- What are some of your learned fears? How do you think you learned them, and when? Who did you learn them from?

- Consider the five Cs of comfort: which one is the most important to you? How does this prioritisation differ in different scenarios?

Key learnings from this chapter

There are five things everyone innately fears a lack of: competence, control, connectedness, consistency and cause.

We learn additional fears as we go through life.

Fear creates an emotional response (and emotions come first and fast).

We can manage fears if we have enough resources.

PART TWO
THE SKILLS TO
BECOME SOUND

We have now covered the science: the neuroscience, physiology and biology underpinning the need to fill our balloons with positive resources. But what are these positive resources? In Part Two, I will share the resources you need to keep your balloon afloat, rising and resilient to rips. You wouldn't take a balloon flight if the balloon wasn't structurally sound. If its ropes were frayed, its canvas thin, and its basket held together with sticky tape and a bit of string from an old tennis racquet, the hot-air balloon would not be fit for purpose. It would be unable to rise, never mind carry you through any inclement weather that it may come across.

The same is true for your brain. We need to make sure it is working to support you, to help you RISE. It needs to be able to accept positive resources, reject negative ones, repair any rips that may occur and navigate life's inevitable challenges. Just like the balloon, it must be SOUND so we can enjoy life's journey, not fear it.

The brain is far more complex than a hot-air balloon; it receives a barrage of information from outside and within us every minute of every day. Some information we are aware of, some we are not. Some we have stored away, some occupy our thoughts all the time. Some information we have misinterpreted, some we disregard and some is just plain wrong. However, the brain does not always distinguish between the different types of information. As far as the brain is concerned, all information is a resource that helps determine whether we are safe or not. That's the brain's job, and it does it well. Too well, sometimes.

As the brain has been programmed to use information as a resource, we can't stop the brain taking in information – nor would we want to, given its success in ensuring the survival of the human race. But we can begin to manage the brain and be more selective as to which information it uses. Applying the principles of SOUND can help the brain use information as a positive resource that supports us rather than a negative one that depletes us.

There are many ways to be SOUND, but this book focuses on four key strategies that have research behind them to support their use in creating positive resources. To be SOUND, you need to apply strategies to the information you take in. These strategies can convert information into a positive resource or prompt you to ignore negative information.

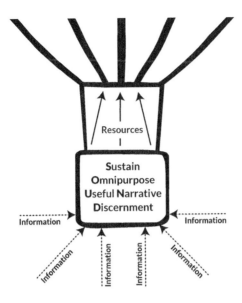

The SOUND filters help you RISE

The four SOUND filters are:

- **S**ustain

- **O**mnipurpose

- **U**seful **N**arrative

- **D**iscernment

The chapters in Part Two dig into each of these elements, offering explanations, activities and toolkits to help you develop the skills to apply the principles of SOUND and enable you to RISE.

4
Sustain

Sustaining the brain is the foundation that lets you RISE. Without ensuring your body and brain are sustainable, it will be almost impossible to apply the other filters, so start here. Just as your body needs the right fuel in the form of nutrients to perform at its best, there are some basics that the brain needs to function at its best (**competence**). This may be boring, but it's true.

We need to look after ourselves by providing the basic resources the body needs to sustain maximum performance, both physically and cognitively. There is no great revelation in the advice to eat well, get eight hours of sleep, exercise and have downtime, but this chapter will show how doing so can add positive resources to your balloon. Without this step, applying all of the other filters in the SOUND model will be tricky. After all, the brain functions on chemical processes, and if we don't have the relevant nutrients to power them, we won't be able to function well. Here are the key means to sustaining ourselves.

Fuel

The brain uses up to 25% of our energy *at rest*, without even doing anything. And, of course, if we are thinking, learning or managing emotions it will use more.

The energy source for the brain is glucose, a form of sugar, but sadly this doesn't mean that gorging on Snickers and Haribo will sustain the brain. As with all the resources we put in the brain, the wrong quantity and quality have a detrimental effect. Refined sugars like the ones you find in chocolate and alcohol have been shown to reduce memory and cause ageing of the brain cells[57] as well as causing type 2 diabetes. You are better off getting your sugar via healthy carbohydrates in vegetables. Sorry about that.

Water also improves brain function, including memory, mood, concentration and our energy levels.[58] Normal water does the trick: no need for 'smart water'. Herbal teas also count as hydrating liquids, but sugary drinks and anything with caffeine or alcohol don't. Given our bodies are 60% water and we lose water daily through peeing, sweating and exhaling, you can see why we are advised to keep it topped up with 1.5–2 litres of water a day.

Eat and drink regularly. Thirst is a message from the brain that our body needs more water; hunger and associated food moods are messages that the body needs fuel. Listen for them and heed their call. If you sustain your brain with nutrients, it can manage the resources that it takes in and our mental well-being.

Sleep

Although sleep patterns vary, we need at least eight hours in a twenty-four-hour period. Young people are considered to be more 'night owls', staying up late and sleeping in. As you age, this changes, which is why your grandparents may start their day at 6am, a time you didn't know existed. Whenever you choose to begin your sleep, you shouldn't finish it until eight hours later. The brain needs this time to do important maintenance.

During the day, all the brain's neurons are working using electrical signals to connect with each other. As with all energy processes, this produces waste matter. When we light a fire to produce heat energy, the waste matter is ash. When we put petrol in a car to produce motion, we get exhaust fumes. When we provide our bodies with food to convert to energy, we get urine and excrement. The process of thinking converts glucose into the electrical charges that power the neurons in the brain. That creates waste matter in the form of toxins, and sleep allows the brain to clean out these toxins as your brain quietens. When you haven't had enough sleep, you get a headache because you still have toxins in your brain.

The brain uses sleep time for filing – filing away memories, archiving some into the long-term memory. This can help with learning: it has been found that sleep strengthens new neurons and connections that have been made in the day and maintains existing ones, trimming some that are less used.[59]

Sleep can help us with insightful thinking. If you have a mental block when trying to solve a problem or be creative, a good technique is to think about it before you fall asleep. The brain continues to process it, but as the 'smart' part of the brain is resting, we are processing without logic limiting our thinking (which is why dreams can be weird: random neurons firing without the control of our logical brain), and we can wake up with creative solutions.

Sleep keeps our brains fit and operating at full power, which we need to RISE. Plus, when we don't have enough sleep we are grumpy, and no one wants to be around a grumpy person.

Exercise

Exercise is not only good for our heart and muscles but excellent for our mental health. Why? Because of the impact of exercise on our brain. Exercise produces chemicals called endorphins in the brain, and these endorphins reduce pain and increase positive feelings. Studies have shown that endorphins can reduce depression,[60] anxiety and stress.[61] The good feelings that endorphins provide can also increase optimism, self-esteem and confidence.[62] There are also studies looking at the role of exercise in repairing neurons – particularly important for research into Alzheimer's and dementia.[63] This is still new work, so watch this space.

You don't have to be a gym bunny to RISE. Just do some activity that raises your heart rate for at least thirty minutes three times a week. Find a fun activity with a 'toward' motivation for you, and you will be more likely to commit to it.

Rest

The brain works by producing electrical signals with different voltages or frequencies measured in Hertz per second: we call them brain waves. Some are rapid, others almost flat.

Imagine going to the gym and just working one arm and nothing else. Eventually you would start to look unbalanced – you'd have a super strong arm, but the rest of you would blow away in a strong wind. Similarly, we need to 'exercise' all the different brain waves to ensure they are all equally fit.

There are five key frequencies in which the brain operates. We use two when the brain is busy: **gamma waves** operate at >35 Hz and occur when there is lots of simultaneous processing going on from different parts of the brain. A higher level of cognitive function fires when we are **investigating** problems, trying to **integrate** multiple or complex pieces of information. This can provide us with those **illuminating** 'lightbulb'/ moments of understanding as information comes together and falls into place. You will be highly alert, maybe even excited. We produce **beta waves** (12–35 Hz) when we are concentrating on specific tasks or solving a particular problem. In this state we are receptive to learning as our attention, memory and information processing are heightened. This frequency signals a sense of awareness and excitement so can be present when we congregate with others or celebrate. It has also been found that exercise can stimulate beta waves.[64]

Frequency	Function	Hz	Pattern
Gamma	• Investigating problems • Integrating multiple or complex pieces of information • Illuminating 'lightbulb' moments	>35 Hz	
Beta	• Educating • Concentrating • Creating • Congregating • Celebrating	12–35 Hz	
Alpha	• Deactivating	8–12 Hz	
Theta	• Contemplating or meditating	4–8 Hz	
Delta	• Sleeping	0.5–4 Hz	

Brain waves

At the gamma and beta frequencies, as you can see in the image, brain waves are rapid and close together – there is a lot of electrical firing going on between neurons! It is hard work, energy sapping and not sustainable, so the brain needs to rest. Even machines have to switch off, but we are not machines and, just to complicate things, there are different types of brain rest. Ideally, we'd do a bit of each of them.

There are three types of brain waves associated with relaxed and restful states.

Alpha waves (8–12 Hz) occur when you are relaxed, in the state before sleep when your mind may be wandering but you are still conscious. This can be a creative time for the brain. It is also a productive state for learning – you are absorbing without concentrating. From a health perspective, being in this state lowers blood pressure and improves production of serotonin (a 'feel good' hormone) and therefore can improve mood. So, the next time you are accused of daydreaming, simply say you are exercising your alpha waves.

From here you can drop into the frequency of **theta waves** (4–8 Hz), when your consciousness is reduced. This brain wave is often studied using Tibetan monks as it is prevalent during meditation, introspection and problem solving. It is during theta that we can often have our best ideas – when we are not thinking about anything specifically. This is because it is during the theta frequency that we can experience bursts of gamma waves – when we bring diverse thoughts and ideas together to create an a-ha! moment. I have seen this state referred to as 'the Tibetan state of conscious-ness' after the monks who are able to induce this state for meditation, relaxation, introspection and uncon-scious problem solving.[65] You can reach this state when doing something that is so automatic you don't even think about it like brushing your teeth or when doing repetitive exercise like running.

Delta waves are the slowest and widest spaced brain waves, operating at 0.5–4 Hz. In this state, we are not aware of our surroundings; we are asleep, maybe dreaming. In addition to the reasons mentioned in the 'Sleep' section, sleep is important because it produces delta waves, which stimulate healing and recovery from illness or injuries and can reduce pain.

The 'ate' model

Ideally, each brain wave type should be 'exercised' every day. This means feeding the brain on a daily basis, making sure it 'ate' everything it needed.

Every day, sati**ate** your hunger by eating well. I am not a nutritionist, but I am sure I won't go far wrong by recommending less sugar, salt and saturated fats. Eat a balanced diet with carbohydrates (the good ones, which include brown grains, not white), protein and fibre. And hydr**ate** with water or non-caffeinated drinks.

Activ**ate** your heart and lungs by exercising, and extri-c**ate** – remove yourself from everyone else at least once a day – to have some alone time. This might involve taking a bath, doing some exercise or reading a book – all without your phone. If the thought of relinquish-ing your phone for just thirty minutes sends you into a panic, giving you palpitations and cold sweats, con-sider that such a physical reaction to the absence of something, even for a short time, is usually associated with addiction or dependency (#justsayin').

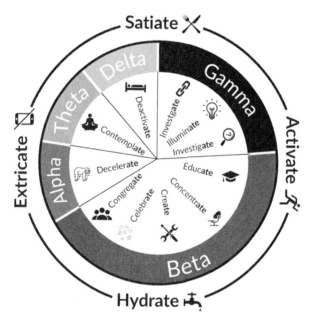

Brain waves and the 'ate' model

Gamma waves are created when we bring together complex data and information, solve difficult problems and enable a solution. It's hard work and sometimes it's hard to come up with an unusual or creative solution on demand. However, one way to activate gamma waves is to actually not think about the problem... I will explain more when we talk about theta waves.

We spend a lot of our day working in the beta frequency. Beta indicates awareness. It's when we are learning, concentrating and creating something. We are also 'aware' when we are interacting socially. Introverts and extroverts alike need interaction with other people, so congregate (socially distanced, if required!) with others.

Be aware that connecting with just anyone is not guaranteed to help sustain your brain. I had a friend, let's call her Lottie, and whenever I went to see her (and it was always me going to see her) I felt exhausted and, frankly, a bit down afterwards. I only noticed when I realised there were days I avoided seeing her or taking her calls – I just didn't have the energy. I realised she was an energy vampire. When we met, she just talked about herself, her work, problems with her boyfriend, her shopping decisions, her week, her month, her year... She never once asked how I was or gave me a chance to talk. It wasn't just a one-off (we all have times when we need these things from our friends), it was *every time* we met. She always needed me to listen to her and talk her problems through, but this constant drama was hard work for me and I realised the relationship was unbalanced. I helped her keep her balloon afloat – but at the cost of mine. I minimised my contact with Lottie, choosing only to see her when my energy was high because she was not good for me.

I have another friend who totally energises me with her positivity, love of life and adventurous spirit, and every time we meet we have fun. She is a great person to have around, and I know if I am down she will always make me feel better. She has been in my life now for more years than either of us dare admit because we are good for each other. I provide a 'sensible head' for her, and we complement each other.

We all have colleagues who are always negative and moaning. Limit your exposure to them and avoid them if you can. Don't let them put those negative resources into your head. One of the most memorable pieces of advice I received was from a boss who was supportive when I was having relationship difficulties. He said, 'Love is like chocolate. You may love it, but it's not good for you.' Sometimes we may love someone, but they are not good for us, and we need to be selective with the people we communicate and connect with as they can dilute our positive resources.

So do something just for fun every day. Maybe even do something that scares you a little – something new and outside of your comfort zone. Then when you have conquered that little fear, celebrate life's little wins!

To relax the brain, be sloth-like and decelerate. Spend some downtime doing a non-taxing activity: watch TV, read a trashy novel, play computer games. We will talk more about reflection in Chapter 8, but reflection is important – whether you meditate or merely contemplate – not just for brain health but for understanding yourself and the world around you. And the more you understand something, the less scary it will be. This is also a critical brain frequency because often, while we are in this state, our best ideas will come to us. Short bursts of gamma waves interrupt theta waves creating those lightbulb moments. So, if you have a difficult problem, think of something else, reflect, meditate or do an activity that puts you in a state where time passes without awareness, like playing the piano or painting.

Finally, deactivate: sleep. I think the human body and the brain are marvellous; however, one of the body's few design flaws is the inability to store sleep. Wouldn't it be great if we could sleep for twenty-four solid hours and then stay awake for three days? Sadly, though, the brain has limited capacity and needs recharging.

To be SOUND, we need to keep the brain healthy, structurally sound and able to do its job. It's boring, but you've got to start with the basics. After reading this chapter, I hope you now have an understanding of the 'why', the science behind the basics of sustaining the brain. You wouldn't put a boxer in the ring without the right training and nutrition and expect them to beat their challenger; similarly, you can't expect your brain to do its job of keeping you safe and managing life's challenges if it's not fit. Like maintaining the hot-air balloon, if it's in good working order, it will enable you to RISE to heights you didn't believe you were capable of before.

ACTIVITY

- Keep a diary of brain basics for a week: when and what you eat, drink and exercise. Note the hours of sleep you get. By writing these down, you become more aware of them. There is a diary template and tips for increasing water consumption and getting better sleep available to downloaded on www.drsammather.com.

- Think about the people you spend your valuable time with. How does each one make you feel: happy, exhausted, stressed, loved, relaxed, intimidated, inferior, safe? Which connections add to your balloon by making you feel good, and which deplete your balloon? Track this in your brain diary.

- After at least a week, reflect on your brain diary. Which areas are you nailing? What do you need to do more of? Which people added resources to your balloon? Which didn't?

- If several things in your life are depleting your balloon, note how you feel. For the next week, feed your brain well, adding only positive resources, then check in with yourself again. How do you feel now? How do the two weeks compare?

Key learnings from this chapter

- Eat well, drink water, exercise and sleep.

- The brain operates at different frequencies (wavelengths) – use them all.

- Look out for energy vampires.

- Take time out, in all its forms.

- Connect and communicate with others.

- Remember the 'ate' model.

5
Omnipurpose

Why are we here? It's a big philosophical question but one that you can answer for yourself.
You are here to be or do whatever you want to. If you
want to do something that is illegal or immoral, you
can, as long as you are prepared to deal with the consequences. As they say, don't do the crime if you can't
do the time.

Omnipurpose ascribes meaning to our actions (**cause**),
helps us gain perspective (**control**), connects us with
others (**connectedness**) and aligns everything we do
(**consistency**). It provides us with positive resources.

Many people go through their entire lives not knowing their purpose – or worse, linking their purpose
to something that will change or disappear, like their

job or even their children. When the job ends or the children leave home, they're left with no direction or reason for being, which can cause mental distress. Research has shown that people who are doing a job they dislike or that is against their values are more prone to depression, poor self-esteem[66] and poorer well-being.[67] Living and working according to your values and purpose increases engagement, satisfaction and performance in one's chosen job.[68] From a psychological perspective, those working in an environment that aligned with their personal values showed reduced cortisol production in response to stressors: they were better able to deal with stress.[69]

What is your omnipurpose, the one reason you are doing what you are doing? And what values determine how you will achieve this omnipurpose? These questions require some consideration, so let me give you some pointers. We'll start with values.

Values

Values are beliefs and morals by which we live our lives – our views on what is right or wrong. They differ from person to person. My niece is vegan, an increasingly popular lifestyle choice. Why did she choose it? It's certainly not because of the availability or price of vegan food (although this is changing). She has chosen to be vegan because of her value system: she believes it is wrong to kill or exploit any animal.

Vegetarians are similar but don't share the same values about foods such as honey, milk or eggs, and they may choose free-range and organic options to ensure the welfare of the animals. This is not to say meat eaters don't have a value system around animals – even meat eaters are often upset at the prospect of people in some countries eating horse, dog or cat.

Values are also cultural. It's OK to catch and eat whales in some countries, while others are opposed to this. Values are also established at a community level; for example, if you are Muslim or Jewish, it would be against your values to eat pork.

Values can also be set at a family level, what you have been taught is right and wrong. Growing up in my house, Sunday lunch involved the whole family sitting at the dining table at 3pm. Every Sunday, no excuse. I hated it at the time and couldn't understand why. But I see now that this was important to my parents as it was the only time we were all in the house at the same time and the only chance we had to talk together as a family.

I worked for a multi-national company, and the office culture in each country was different. I used to enjoy the Paris office because the lunches were so civilised! You took a full hour, wine was available with the amazing food that was served, and it was sociable. In fact, our French colleagues were shocked and somewhat disgusted that the norm in the London office was to grab a sandwich from the canteen and take it back to your desk to eat in front of your emails.

Interesting that I have focused on food-based examples. It must be lunchtime as I write this. (See how clever the brain is?)

Think of some of your values. What do you believe is right and wrong? To what extent does your workplace reflect your values? You may feel that there is something about your work that you don't like but you're not sure why. It could be a misalignment of your values. If you value collaboration but the leaders in your workplace are more dictatorial, your brain will be trying to flag this discrepancy to you in the form of feelings: discomfort, embarrassment, outrage.

When you feel your values are being undermined, the brain will inform you there is a threat ahead. If you were working somewhere that didn't match your values, your brain's balloon would have lots of rips in it as you frantically tried to balance what's being asked of you and what you believe in. Would you work for a nuclear power company? A gambling or pay-day-loan company? An airline?

We also have internal values about ourselves, and they determine how we wish to be treated and how we treat others. If you know when your values are not being upheld (and your balloon is being depleted), you can do something about it.

In a former job, I was asked to make some people redundant, but not for the right reasons. There were personality clashes between my boss and the people he wanted me to let go, and he wanted me to do his dirty work. There was little legal reason to make them redundant. I felt terrible about this, and I was worrying, not sleeping and eating too much chocolate. My values were being compromised in two ways: my boss was not taking accountability or responsibility for his issues, and I felt that it was not an honest or fair process. These were people's lives he wanted me to mess with. I refused. I then resigned. I don't want to work for a company that is so devious and underhanded – it's just not who I am. A discrepancy between the person you are and who you have to be at work can lead to feelings of dejection, shame, embarrassment and even feeling threatened.[70] I was deploying valuable psychological resources in being someone I wasn't (a devious, unfair jerk), and the resulting emotions created negative resources which deflated my balloon.

It's important to know what's important to you. I run sessions with leaders who have over forty years' experience and who are still not aware of their personal values. When we do the exercise, they realise that certain events upset them or made them angry because they went against their personal values. In this chapter, I offer you the chance to explore your values.

Our behaviours are the expression of our attitudes.
Our attitudes are driven by our values and beliefs.

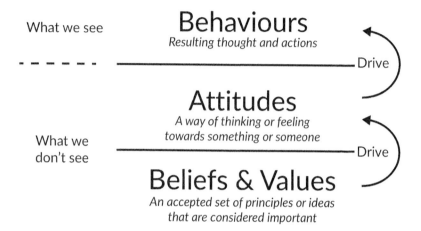

What we see

Behaviours
Resulting thought and actions

Drive

Attitudes
*A way of thinking or feeling
towards something or someone*

What we
don't see

Drive

Beliefs & Values
*An accepted set of principles or ideas
that are considered important*

The Behaviour, Attitudes, Beliefs & Values model

In one former workplace, the dress code was a source
of conflict between two colleagues. One believed that
we should wear formal office wear (suits, shirts, etc);
the other believed we should be allowed to wear jeans
and t-shirts. It became quite an issue, each moaning
about the other's 'crazy ideas about clothes'. Both
individuals had strong values about being seen as
professional and an expert in their field. Whereas my
colleague who wore a suit believed that profession-
alism is reflected in not only what you do but how
you look, my jeans-wearing colleague believed that
the outputs and quality of work determined your
expertise, not how you looked. Same values, different
beliefs, different behaviours.

Note: beliefs are not necessarily factually true. After all, people used to believe the world was flat. **But one's beliefs are true for them**, and they can be difficult to change. As my fashion-diverse colleagues demonstrated, beliefs and values are not wrong or right; they have just been shaped over the individual's lifetime by society, culture, family and/or their own experience.

Whenever you see a behaviour in someone, consider what the value or belief is that's driving that behaviour. One day, I was walking through my local town – a quaint English market town. On the other side of the road were three girls around fifteen years old. They were being loud. One of them then drop-kicked a large cup of thick milkshake from a popular burger takeaway. The milkshake splattered all over the road, and the empty and smashed cup rolled away, settling a metre from a waste bin. The girls laughed and walked away. I was *incensed*.

I crossed the road towards them, pointed to the battered cup and said, 'Excuse me, I think you have forgotten to put that in the bin'. The three girls looked at me with hate in their eyes. 'What?' asked the loudest of the three and perpetrator of the milkshake drop-kick. Still pointing to the cup, I replied, 'I said, I think you have forgotten to put that in the bin'. The thought crossed my mind that maybe I was about to be stabbed. Never taking her eyes off me, the loud girl picked up the cup and resentfully put it in the bin.

'Thank you,' I said. As I walked away, the girls hurled verbal abuse at me, but I was OK with that. Sticks and stones and all that.

When telling my friends about this, they thought I was crazy, exclaiming, 'You might have got stabbed!' I scoffed, declining to mention I'd had the same thought. 'What on earth possessed you?' they asked.

Good question. What did possess me? There are things that happen every day that I don't react to: terrible drivers, rude shop assistants or people in mobility scooters running you down on the pavement. So why this incident?

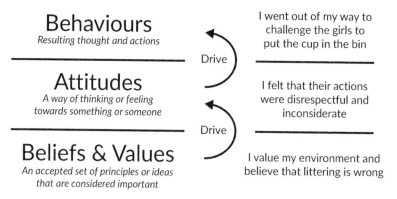

Behaviours, Attitudes, Beliefs & Values applied

Using the Behaviour, Beliefs, Values model, I reflected that my values were so offended at the girls' behaviour that I felt I had to do something. I realised I was annoyed because I love the town I live in; I value its English quaintness and prettiness. My environment is important to me. (I am so house proud that my home looks like a show home – with the added advantage of cat hairs.) These girls had shown no respect for the environment or even basic littering laws. Plus, they were shouty, which showed a lack of respect for others and also annoyed me.

Respect is clearly an important value for me. What about you? What are your values? It's not for me to pre-scribe them, and they do change as you go through life (if you have children, consider what your values were before they came along), but the following activity can get you thinking about what's important to you now.

ACTIVITY: VALUES

1. Think of a recent behaviour that stemmed from an emotional response. Work backwards through the Behaviour, Attitudes, Beliefs & Values model to find the value beneath the behaviour.
2. In Appendix 1, there are a list of twenty-seven value words along with spaces for you to add your own (they are your values, after all).
   - Step 1: Identify twelve of the most meaningful words to you.
   - Step 2: Narrow these down to six.
   - Step 3: Define what each of these six means to you.

Remember these definitions like a moral code: how you want to be treated and how you are prepared to treat others. It might be productive to do this activity with a group of friends. Getting others' input is always useful in helping broaden thinking.

This activity is also available for download from www.drsammather.com.

Purpose

What is our purpose? From a biological perspective, it's continuing the species; however, more and more people are choosing to remain childfree, which can be a values-driven choice. In a 2018 *New York Times* poll, a third of Americans of childbearing age cited climate change as a reason to have fewer children.[71] If your purpose is not to bear offspring, what is it?

To be prepared to invest psychological resources into an activity, we need to understand why we are doing it – the '**cause**' part of our Rock of Fear. Doing something that has no purpose is soul destroying over time and can affect our mental health. Pointless tasks used to be used as a punishment for prisoners. The phrase 'money for old rope' has come from one of those tasks: prisoners were asked to unpick the strands of a rope, only to make it into rope again. Another job was 'the crank', which the prisoner had to turn a certain number of times a day. The crank didn't do anything, they just had to turn it. The prison officers could tighten a screw to increase the resistance of the crank, making the pointless job harder. That's how prison officers got the name 'screws'. To help us see what we do as more than a daily grind with no reward, we need to understand its purpose.

A Japanese study of over 40,000 people aimed to determine the psychological factors that contributed to longevity.[72] It was discovered that those who had a purpose lived significantly longer than those who did not. Without a purpose, the mortality rate increased, irrespective of causes of death. The authors of this study considered that this was because having a purpose gave people a reason for living. Not every purpose had this effect, though – only purposes that 'made life worth living'. This type of purpose improved a quality of life, and gave life meaning. My research also showed that the development of a purpose increased feelings of well-being and resilience, but that the nature of the purpose was important.[73]

For those who have not considered this concept, when I first ask them what their purpose is they will often respond with their job title. I then ask why they do their jobs. Often the response is 'money'. Well, that can't be true. If money was the only reason they worked, they would choose a better-paid – perhaps even illegal or immoral – profession: smuggling drugs, prostitution or politics.

So there is something more than money involved. Money may be a means to help you reach your purpose, but I'll give you a hint: your purpose is rarely to gain material wealth. You might get it on the way, but if you don't, that's OK because you are still living your purpose and living your purpose makes you happy.

Your purpose may change throughout your life or it can remain constant, but it needs to be overarching – bigger than things that might not be around forever. If you see your purpose as your job, you will feel you have lost your purpose if you lose your job. Similarly, people often cite raising children as a purpose, but while it certainly will be their focus for a good eighteen years it is not their purpose. Kids will (hopefully) leave home eventually and may go on to have their own families. What will your purpose be then? With an overarching purpose, everything you do contributes to it: your job, raising a family, your hobbies. They are not your purpose – they are ways to achieve your purpose.

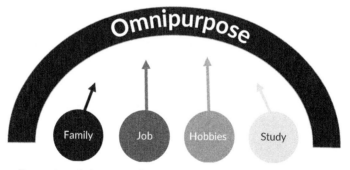

Examples of elements that contribute to your Omnipurpose

My purpose is to enable others to learn and grow. No matter what my job is, as long as I am enabling others to learn and grow I am fulfilling my purpose. My jobs have been many: trainer, lecturer, coach, researcher, talent leader, author, student, consultant, aerobics instructor, shelf stacker and call centre operative. The job title is unimportant; as long as it allows me scope to meet my purpose I will find happiness.

I have a friend who is lucky enough not to need to work, but she doesn't sit around watching *Neighbours* or *Loose Women*. She has an objective in her life that gives it meaning. She is committed to improving the lives of women through education. Many years ago, when travelling through Cambodia, she saw first-hand how poverty impacted education, particularly for girls. Moved by this, she returned home and researched further, discovering this is prevalent in many poor countries. In learning about the positive impacts of educating girls – not only for the girls, but also for their families and the country's economy – she has made it her life goal to improve this situation. Everything she does is about empowering girls. Yes, she still has to do mundane things; sometimes when money is tight she gets a part-time job working on a supermarket checkout, but even then she is living her purpose. It drives the way she communicates with others, how and where she spends her money, and how she raises her daughter and son. They are all means to a greater purpose. She is making a difference.

Your purpose does not have to change the world. You may be familiar with the story of the starfish by Loren Eiseley; one day a man was walking along a beach and discovered millions of starfish washed up on the shore. He starts picking them up one by one and throwing them back into the sea. Someone spots him doing this and says, 'What are you doing? There are so many starfish, you aren't going to make much of a difference.' Picking up another starfish and throwing it back into the sea, the man says, 'Well, I'm making a difference to this one'.

It took me years to realise my purpose. I had to find out what I was good at and what I enjoyed in life. The Ikigai model, below, can help you determine this. The model has four components:

1. What are you good at?

I believe you can be good at everything – after all, we all have the same brains – but there are some things that we can be good at with less effort than others. Find out what these things are for you. It may take you some time to discover them, and during the process you may have to do a lot of things that you'll find difficult to be good at, but that's OK – you are on the journey.

If something makes you feel good, this is a clue that you might be good at it. Feedback from others is also an indicator: if people are giving you positive feed-back about it, then you may be good at it. My friend was always top of the class in maths. She enjoyed it and didn't have to put much effort into getting high scores: it just seemed obvious to her. She chose to become an accountant – doing what she was good at. But being good at something is not enough…

2. What can you be paid for?

Another reason for my friend pursuing accountancy is that she knew she could earn money doing it. Teachers and parents encouraged her to choose that field – a sensible piece of advice. She was showing an aptitude for numbers that could make her financially secure, but being good at accountancy and the good pay still weren't enough. She still had feelings of discontent and boredom.

3. What does the world need?

There is no doubt we need accountants. They are never out of work. My friend therefore found something she was good at, something she could be paid for and something in demand. Excellent. So, has she found her purpose? No, for two reasons.

The first reason is, for you to find your purpose, you also need to love what you do.

4. What do you love?

There are things we can be good at but don't enjoy doing. I am good at running, perhaps so good I could get paid for it and represent my country, but I hate it. It hurts and it's boring, which is pretty much how my friend feels about accountancy. I have even met doctors who are doing their job because they liked biology, it's a secure job and the world needs doctors, but they don't love being a doctor. What they have is a profession and a vocation, but there is no passion.

The Ikigai model requires you to have balance between these four elements: gaining a profession, a vocation (job), a mission and a passion. Research has shown that if you can achieve all four of these, then irrespective of how much you earn, what car you drive and what material goods you have, you will have a happier and more content life – a life with a purpose.[74]

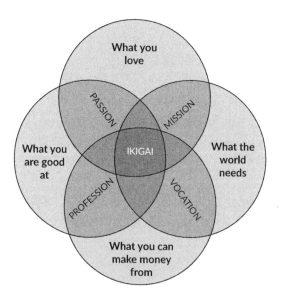

The Ikigai model

Let's say our accountant and doctors did love their jobs and they met all the requirements of the Ikigai model. Would their jobs be their purposes? No. As we said above, your job is not your purpose, and this is the second reason that my accountant friend did not find her purpose from doing a job that she was good at, that paid well and that was in demand. Your purpose is higher than your job. Famous people – pop stars, actors, reality stars – are a good example of this concept. They are often doing what they love and are good at, they earn (lots of) money from it, and apparently the world needs reality stars; yet, many suffer from mental health problems, asking themselves, 'What's the meaning of it all?' As a result, they often seek activities that give them a more meaningful purpose than having Ferraris in the drive and a boat at St Tropez.

Robbie Williams found fame, fortune and adoration (particularly from me) through the band Take That and subsequently as a successful solo singer. He also found a prescription drug addiction and depression until he began to focus on something other than himself.

Robbie Williams loves football. He was (at one time) good at football, and he is also good at networking and inspiring people to a bigger purpose. Money for UNICEF is something the world needs, so Robbie Williams started Soccer Aid. He doesn't get paid for it, but he doesn't need to. Involving himself in this charity gave him meaning and purpose. He is making a difference to others.

To find your purpose, we need to dig deeper than a job. Returning to the example of my accountant friend, we know she is good with numbers. When I ask her what she does like about her job, she explains that when there is a problem with the books and the numbers don't tally, she likes being able to investigate and solve the problem. She finds the stuff about reporting, maintaining expenses and submitting tax forms less stimulating – doing that day in and day out depletes the resources in her balloon.

My friend is good at and loves solving numerical problems and spotting trends or irregularities. She says that's the fun part. I'll take her word for it. She gets great satisfaction from finding anomalies and presenting a solution using numbers. It makes her feel like she has done something someone else hasn't (**competence**) and that she has made a difference (**cause**) by helping someone (**connectedness**).

While my friend doesn't like the specific job of accountancy, an activity within the job makes her feel good and puts positive resources into her balloon. Whatever job she has, as long as she is able to solve problems using numbers and data she will be meeting the 'good at' and 'love' parts of her Ikigai: her purpose. My friend's purpose is to help others solve problems using data, and asking 'Where does the world need this and how can she make money from it?' opens up a world of opportunities – not just in terms of work but in terms of how she helps others and the contribution she makes to the world. Some of these options may not pay as much as accountancy, but she would be happier with a fuller balloon.

Whatever you choose to do in life, make sure you are doing what you love and something you are good at. This will add positive resources to your balloon, keeping it afloat and helping you maintain your resilience. Yes, I know we tie ourselves to jobs we hate because we have fancy cars, mortgages and designer gear to buy. These are what trap us and deplete our resources. If I were coaching you, I would be looking to understand what fears the fancy cars, mortgage or designer gear are trying to quell and what the beliefs and values are that are fuelling this (again, #justsayin').

ACTIVITY: FINDING YOUR PURPOSE

1. Write down three activities that you do in a normal week or month. They may be activities you have to do (like going to work) or ones that you choose to do (like going to the gym).
2. Consider what you like about each activity (you may say you hate work but there will be *something* about it you like: meeting friends, the lasagne on a Wednesday).
3. Be specific about what you like and why.

4. Do this a few times and see if there is a common thread in what you like to do.

5. Now look at the common thread. Does it make you feel good? Does it add to your balloon? If so, you are beginning to shape your overarching objective.

I have put a couple of examples in the following image to get you started. This exercise is also available for download from www.drsammather.com.

Key learnings from this chapter

- Learn to understand the source of your behaviour: your values and beliefs.

- Evaluate your values and beliefs: did you decide them or have you just taken on those of the people around you?

- Having purpose and an overarching objective helps put the world in perspective and can help you live a longer and happier life.

- Find out what you are passionate about: this fills your balloon, so do more of it.

6
Useful Narrative

In Chapter 4, we talked about how the brain is constantly on the lookout to ensure we move towards **consistency**, **connectedness**, **control**, **competence** and **cause**. If there is a threat to any of these, the brain quickly sends a warning to us in the form of emotions, which, being the clever beings we are, we articulate and describe to ourselves as thoughts. Because this happens so quickly, they turn into automatic thoughts. These become our internal voice that provides a narrative to our lives.

We all have that internal voice, the one that says, 'Everyone is staring at that spot on my nose' or 'I don't think he likes me' or 'One day they are going to find out I am just winging this' (imposter syndrome). You may not voice these thoughts externally – you may go to great lengths to convince the world that you are not thinking these things – but your brain knows. Your internal voice keeps reminding you.

One of the most powerful realisations I have ever had was that **I don't have to believe everything my brain tells me**. It's designed to protect me but sometimes the messages it sends are a bit over-zealous and sometimes they are outdated or simply wrong. Our automatic thoughts can end up disseminating self-doubt, insecurity and fear, deflating our balloon. Our brains can, and do, lie to us. Or at least misinterpret and exaggerate. The brain's intent is good, but the execution can be heavy-handed. By being aware of our automatic thoughts and internal narrative, we can control them, rather than them controlling us. To keep our balloon afloat, we need to make sure our automatic thoughts create a useful narrative.

Having a useful narrative lets us take **control** of the information around us, ensuring that it promotes our **competence** and maximises our positive resources. The bad news is, because they happen so quickly, we can't stop automatic thoughts, at least not without effort and practice. But we can recognise them when they happen and then challenge them. The following section offers techniques, and advice on implementing them, to help change negative automatic thoughts into positive thoughts, adding resources to your balloon.

The Ladder of Inference

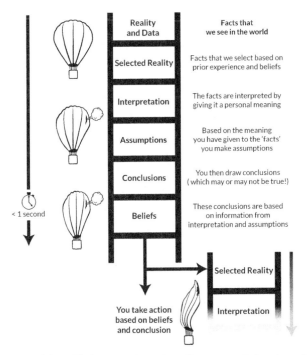

The Ladder of Inference, based on the concept developed by Chris Argyris (1970) and described in P Senge, The Fifth Discipline: The Art and Practice of the Learning Organization (Random House, 1992)

First, let's examine the automatic thought process that happens in less than a second, using the Ladder of Inference. The Ladder of Inference above shows the steps the brain can take to go from an event (facts) to an action that we take. These steps take us down the ladder, depleting resources as we go. The process can then lead us down additional ladders, further reducing our resources.

One night, I had invited my boyfriend over to my house for a home-cooked supper. Cooking is not my favourite thing, so this was a big deal for me. I had spent the whole day preparing. I told him to be at mine by 8pm, scheduling the food to be ready then.

However, 8.15 ticked past and no boyfriend. Another fifteen minutes passed – no boyfriend and the starter was now burnt. By 8.45, the main course was fit only for the bin. When he eventually turned up at 9pm, I responded with lots of shouting, crying and throwing of plates while I threw him out and told him it was over, we were finished!

My boyfriend was somewhat perplexed, acknowledging that, yes, he was late but there was a good reason, and being one hour late was hardly grounds for finishing a relationship. What had happened? During the hour I spent waiting for him, I had descended down the ladder of inference so many times I had created a narrative that worked me into quite the frenzy. And this is how…

Had he arrived when I decided that our relationship was over, I might have taken action, but no. My emotions were running the show now, and his continued absence allowed me to descend another ladder.

I realise that writing this process down makes me look pretty irrational, but remember, these were automatic thoughts and the process took about a second. Then I spent an hour mulling over and reinforcing this narrative. Each time I stepped down a rung on the ladder, I created a rip in my balloon.

I had been stressed out. Like I said, cooking is not a relaxing activity for me. It depletes my resources. Each time I moved down the ladder, I created another rip in my balloon, resulting in even fewer cognitive resources available to deploy the logic needed to prevent any further descent into despair.

Later, having calmed down and ordered in a take-away to replace the incinerated meal, there was time for reflection. Had my limbic system (emotions) not been running the show due to the pressures of using such a complicated piece of machinery as an oven, I would have been able to use my logical brain to challenge myself and halt my descent down the ladder(s). I could have looked for evidence to support or disprove these thoughts, which would have changed my narrative and I don't think I would have got past the first rung. Is he really 'always' late? No, not always. He is sometimes late, but there is usually a good reason, and I would interpret that he was late for a good reason. End of descent. End of drama.

This is why people tell you to 'go away and calm down' when you're upset. Sometimes you can only form rational thoughts when you step off the ladder. When your brain sends you a message in the form of a negative emotion – anger, fear, upset – and you

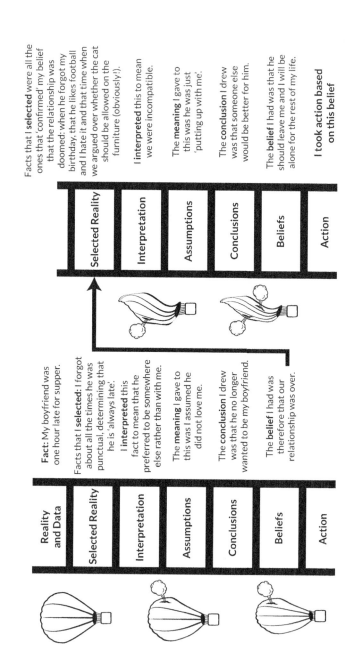

Reality and Data

Fact: My boyfriend was one hour late for supper.

Selected Reality

Facts that I **selected**: I forgot about all the times he was punctual, determining that he is 'always late'.

Interpretation

I **interpreted** this fact to mean that he preferred to be somewhere else rather than with me.

Assumptions

The **meaning** I gave to this was I assumed he did not love me.

Conclusions

The **conclusion** I drew was that he no longer wanted to be my boyfriend.

Beliefs

The **belief** I had was therefore that our relationship was over.

Action

Selected Reality

Facts that I **selected** were all the ones that 'confirmed' my belief that the relationship was doomed: when he forgot my birthday, that he likes football and I hate it and that time when we argued over whether the cat should be allowed on the furniture (obviously!).

Interpretation

I **interpreted** this to mean we were incompatible.

Assumptions

The **meaning** I gave to this was he was just 'putting up with me.'

Conclusions

The **conclusion** I drew was that someone else would be better for him.

Beliefs

The **belief** I had was that he should leave me and I will be alone for the rest of my life.

Action

I took action based on this belief

The first ladder of inference for my ruined supper

sense you are balancing at the top of the ladder, step off by distancing yourself from whatever your brain is interpreting as a threat. When the adrenaline and cortisol have disappeared and you feel calmer, your smart brain comes back online and you can challenge each step of the ladder.

Managing the Ladder of Inference

Ladder	Example	Ask and Challenge...
Reality and Data	My boyfriend was one hour late for supper.	**Ask:** What happened? FACTS and evidence only
Selected Reality	Facts that I selected: I forgot about all the times he was punctual, determining that he is 'always late'.	**Ask:** What part of the facts have you omitted or elaborated on? **Challenge**: ALWAYS late? Can you think of times he was on time?
Interpretation	I interpreted this fact to mean that something else was more important than me.	**Ask:** Why have you chosen to interpret it this way? **Challenge:** How else could you interpret the facts?
Assumptions	The meaning I gave to this was that clearly, he did prefer to be somewhere else.	**Ask:** What assumptions are you making? **Challenge:** What else could it mean if you just looked at the facts in the first step?

Continued

Managing the Ladder of Inference (cont.)

Ladder	Example	Ask and Challenge...
Conclusions	The conclusion I drew was that he did not love me.	**Ask:** What evidence do you have to back this up? **Challenge:** Has there ever been a time when this conclusion would not be true?
Beliefs	Therefore, the belief I had was that our relationship was doomed.	**Ask:** What facts/ evidence do you have? **Challenge:** What else might be driving this belief?
Actions		**Ask:** The action you are about to take, is it based on reality and data or emotions? **Challenge:** Manage your overzealous limbic system!

ACTIVITY: LADDERS

Part 1: Retracing Your Steps

Consider the last time you lost control emotionally. Let's look at the process using the ladder. Start by writing down the 'action you took' at the bottom of the ladder, and consider how you were feeling at the time.

Then, go to the top of the ladder. With no judgement, write the fact of what happened. Someone might have asked you to do something, or made a comment, or not completed a process at work correctly.

Then go down the remaining rungs of the ladder, writing down your thoughts and feelings at the time of the incident.

Part 2: Changing the Narrative

For steps 3–7, challenge each of these thoughts using logic, evidence and fact. Even if you find a fact to support your view, are you able to also find facts to disprove it? Create a balance and generate alternative options.

Think about how this balance feels. You may still be annoyed but perhaps less so. Even if someone else was in the wrong, why should your balloon suffer? In applying the smart part of your brain and creating alternative scenarios, you are taking control of your own cognitive resources by preventing or repairing rips in your balloon.

Also, consider the other person's intent. I choose to believe that people are essentially good. They may be trying to protect themselves, but they are not deliberately setting out to hurt you.

If I'd been paying attention to myself during my supper drama, there was a clue my emotions were taking over at the first step. Had I listened to it, there might have been less drama and no need for a visit to IKEA for a new dinner set.

The alarm bell was the word 'always' in 'He is always late'. This is a generalisation. When I asked myself if my boyfriend was always late, I had to say no. He wasn't always late, just sometimes. Other generalisation words include: every (every time, everyone, everyday), never, none, all, no one, should, must, good and bad. These words suggest something or someone is either one thing or another: they are binary.

Binary thinking creates judgements that have one of two outcomes. Events, things and people are either good or bad, right or wrong. Everything is either black or white.

Always	vs	Never
All/Every	vs	None
Should	vs	Should not
Must	vs	Must not
Good	vs	Bad
Right	vs	Wrong
Black	vs	White

Binary Thinking

This is a tough way to think about things, especially yourself, because a negative judgement can deplete your resources and sink your balloon. It can also lead to stereotypes as there is no room for anything other than two options: 'Salespeople will do anything to get the deal', 'Finance will always say no', 'The IT department are a bunch of introverted nerds'. There are times when these beliefs may be right, but not for all salespeople, not for all finance teams, not for all IT people.

What if there were more than two options? Rather than only good and bad or black and white, there are a range of perspectives. Taking a 'perspective of plenty' allows you to look at things from multiple angles and see all options and alternatives.

Perspective of plenty

A perspective of plenty is being able to see a situation or issue from multiple perspectives with multiple solutions. In doing so you can identify the perspective that adds to the resources in your balloon, rather than depletes them. You might see lockdown as 'bad' (binary viewpoint) or you could say, 'there are some aspects of lockdown that are not good, but there are some that are not so bad; I can write a book, learn a language, get to another level on FIFA 21, or complete the health and safety e-learnings I was supposed to do three months ago.' In choosing the latter, you are changing the narrative about lockdown in a way which preserves your resources by making the situation less scary.

Always	Frequently	Occasionally	Rarely	Never
All/Every	Most	Some	Few	None
Should	Could	May	Might	Should not
Must	Ideal	Recommend	Advised	Must not
Good	Favourable	Reasonable	Flawed	Bad
Right	Proper	Expected	Different	Wrong
Black	Pewter	Slate	Silver	White

Perspective of plenty

At work, perhaps there is a merger taking place. Scary stuff. There is uncertainty everywhere. You can take a binary approach – 'I will either have a job or I won't because they will fire me' – or take a perspective of plenty, recognising that there are more than two options. 'What opportunities could this bring that I might want to take advantage of, such as moving departments, a promotion or redundancy?' (Yes, redundancy can be, and often is, an opportunity.)

Unfortunately, a lot of life's structure is binary: we are told from an early age what is 'good' and what is 'bad' (usually in the context of behaviour). This is sad because when a two-year-old is not doing as they are told, they are labelled 'bad' when what they are doing is important developmentally: exploring the world as an individual entity separate from their parents. It's not bad behaviour, it's good behaviour. It just didn't suit Mum or Dad at the time.

At school, we are boxed into categories: sporty, brainy, a swot, a nerd, cool, not cool. My sister and I are close in age so were constantly compared at school. One year, I didn't do as well as her in running the 100m, so I was dubbed 'not sporty'. Having been told that, I believed it, opting out of sport using as many excuses as I could come up with: dodgy knees, forgotten kit, feeling ill, dog ate my hockey stick. After all, why would I do something I am no good at? I studied instead. This got me good grades, while my sister continued to spend her time on the athletics field getting better and better running times. Throughout our school years, she was the 'sporty' one and I was the 'brainy' one, which is utter nonsense. We are given binary labels which we then live up (or down) to. As it turns out, my sister is as 'brainy' as me and I am as just as sporty as her.

School compares students using grades, each of which has a value: A = good, D = bad. We pass or fail exams. The world of work is the same: we are performing or we aren't; we are 'competent' or 'not competent'. All these are binary measures and judgements, and all of them can deplete our resources and sink our balloon.

Imagine if I had been told that I wasn't running the 100m as fast as my sister *yet* that I was capable of it and the PE teacher Miss 'It's-only-snow-get-out-there-girls' worked with me to achieve it. What if my boss told me she was going to give me a low performance appraisal score but it just meant I hadn't mastered this competency *yet*? Taking a perspective of plenty helps us find unique alternatives, what else does this tell me? I still have some work to do, but **my score is not an indication of my capability**. We are all capable of the same things – our brains all function in similar ways.

The belief that we are all able to achieve whatever we put our mind to stems from Carol Dweck's 'growth mindset' idea.[75] Dweck started her professional life working with children, realising that toddlers are not discouraged if they don't achieve something. If a toddler struggles to balance one brick on top of another and the top one keeps falling off, they keep trying again, learning each time. They don't decide after the first time the brick topples off that they 'aren't good at brick balancing' and toddle away from the task, never to pick up a brick again. Imagine if that happened – we would learn nothing! Dweck noticed that the toddlers persevered unencumbered by fear, disappointment and labels. Then, as we grow, something changes. We begin to compare ourselves with others: friends, siblings, TV characters, the media, parental values, societal values, corporate values, bosses and colleagues. And we begin to feel scared. We question our **competence**, judging it 'good' or 'bad'. We feel safer if we don't do anything that results in a 'bad' judgement, and thus we limit ourselves.

We strive to 'fit in', to be like others to alleviate our **connectedness** fear, so we conform, limiting ourselves to what others think we should be. I am currently on a campaign for grey hair. I've had grey hairs since I was thirty, but of course they have increased over the years. That's perfectly normal, yet I have been led to believe that grey hairs (on a woman!) are bad. For decades, I have been spending a lot of money putting a factory's worth of chemicals on my head to hide this natural process. Why? Because at some point the media and society decided that men looked 'distinguished' with grey hair and women just looked old. And I fell for it. But no more – I am #ditchingthedye. I have some grey hair. It's not good. It's not bad. It just is.

ACTIVITY: WHAT'S YOUR PERSPECTIVE?

Now might be a good time for an activity to see how much you limit your thinking and whether you have a perspective of plenty. Complete the perspective of plenty questionnaire in Appendix 2 or download it from www.drsammather.com.

The perspective of plenty questionnaire will likely have revealed some limiting beliefs and some less limiting ones. That's ok. We all have a bit of both. In the areas where you have a more binary perspective try reframing it, looking at the issue differently.

Let's take question 1 in the questionnaire: *'You are in a meeting and several people are discussing something you know nothing about'*. If you scored 'A', try to balance your view by writing down the fears and then add 'but':

Binary thinking		Reframe with
I am afraid I should know what they are on about		I won't know if I don't ask
They are cleverer than me	*But*	That means I can learn a lot from them
I will look stupid		If I ask about it appropriately, I won't

Perspective of plenty questionnaire question 1 reframing

By looking for alternatives between the black and white, the good and bad, we become less self-critical and more open to new experiences. This helps turn a perspective that might deplete our resources into one that maintains our resources, keeping our balloon afloat.

There are some key principles that can help you adopt a perspective of plenty:

- **Trust that everything happens for a reason**

We might not know the reason now, or next week or even next year, but everything provides a lesson to help us grow and reach our potential. As a child, my family moved to different regions approximately every four years due to my dad's job. At the time, I hated it. Being the new girl with a strange accent sometimes made school challenging. But now I can see that it taught me valuable skills, such as being able to start conversations with strangers and switch accents easily. I have also learned that you can make a home anywhere, an attitude which helped me live and work all over the world.

- **Setbacks and mistakes are just feedback**

If things haven't gone to plan, it's just a message telling us that we need to do something differently. Our job is to discover what that is and try again, even if we still don't get the outcome we wanted. It's all just feedback. Take my cooking – every hard-in-the-middle baked potato teaches me what I need to be doing differently (it's usually patience and planning). Mistakes I made at work are all lessons which have made me better at my job.

- **Embrace challenges**

A challenge may involve doing new things, or it may mean building upon something you have done before. And yes, this may take you to the limits of your capability, outside your comfort zone. That is where the magic stuff happens; we learn, grow and gain more resources.

Learning and developing new skills to overcome challenges will take you beyond what you are currently able to do. If you only did things that you knew you could do, staying in your comfort zone, you would never learn to drive, never learn a new sport, never get a job... never *live*.

- **Effort is essential**

Moving out of that comfort zone, learning something new, doesn't just happen. We can't get to the top of our game without the effort of getting up when we fall down, trying again and carrying on. Anyone who tells you otherwise is lying. Ask any top sportsperson, businessperson, actor, singer, *anyone*, and they will say success takes hard work. There are no shortcuts, and thank goodness, because effort is essential to learning and growing, and...

- **Skills come from hard work**

Effort and skills are connected. The good news is that if skills come from effort, we can all improve our skills in whatever we do. When I started my PhD, I was terrified of statistics. Having decided I was 'no good at maths', I was afraid of the amount of statistical analysis I needed to do to get my doctorate. But I wasn't going to let this stop me. I got a book on statistics and worked my way through it page by page. It was hard. Sometimes I was confused and had to ask for help, but I persevered. I now have more statistical analysis skill than I had when I started. Would I now call myself a statistician? Nope, but I stepped out of my maths comfort zone and gained more skills. And if I needed to do it again, I know I could.

- **Everything can be fixed**

Well, death is pretty final, but everything else can be undone or at least fixed. So things didn't go as planned. Make amends. Change the outcome. Got on the wrong train? Get off and turn around. Accidentally 'emailed–all' your boss's holiday plans? Apologise (a lot), fix it, reflect on what went wrong, learn from it and don't do it again. Lost your temper with your friend and called him a pompous negaton? Apologise. Nothing is permanent.

Adopting a perspective of plenty will help your balloon stay afloat by creating positive resources.

ACTIVITY: APPLYING THE PERSPECTIVE OF PLENTY

A picture of the wheel of life is available from www.drsammather.com. It is a common tool used in coaching to help people assess their lives and what needs to change. We are going to use it to help you apply the perspective of plenty.

To complete the wheel of life, grade how happy you are with each of the areas of your life from 0–10. A 0 means you are very unhappy with it and a 10 means very happy. If there is an area that is not relevant to you, or there is something you would like included, then remove, add or replace as you wish – it's your wheel of life!

Rate each area by drawing a line at each level. It should look something like this:

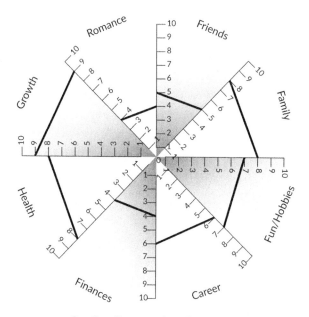

Grading lines on the wheel of life

From this person's wheel, we can see that the areas of their life that they are least happy with are Romance, Friends, Career and Finances.

For each of your low-scoring areas, write down a belief you have about that area, then think about which fear this is playing to. Rewrite the belief using a perspective of plenty.

To be clear, the perspective of plenty doesn't in itself solve problems, but in creating more positive alternatives, it enables you to at least maintain your resource level. Where current beliefs are negative, they create rips in your balloon, causing you to lose valuable cognitive resources and your balloon to sink.

The perspective of plenty positions the situation as temporary (because everything is temporary) and fixable. Framed this way, they are less likely to create rips and may even add positive resources to your balloon. This framing enables you to maintain sufficient resources to change the ratings on your wheel of life.

Sometimes it's hard to apply a perspective of plenty because it requires effort: your brain needs the resources in the first place to be able to manage the thoughts that are so well engrained in your neurons, they appear automatically – as the argument with my boyfriend demonstrated. The key is noticing when these thoughts pop into your head and converting them from a destructive narrative to a useful narrative by creating alternative and plentiful options.

Key learning from this chapter

🎈 Seeing things in binary 'black and white' can deplete our resources

🎈 Applying a perspective of plenty creates new and unique perspectives

🎈 A perspective of plenty maintains or even creates resources in our balloon

7
Discernment

'Discernment: the ability to recognise details, accurately tell the difference between similar things and make intelligent judgements by using such observations.'[76]

With the exception of death, we have a choice in every aspect of life. Even with death, we can sometimes make choices that influence the how and when of it. You may not like the look of option B, but at least it is an option. You choose how you live your life, what you believe in, who you are friends with, what you wear, whether you stay at work, how you respond to situations and where you focus your attention. Deliberately making choices increases our sense of **control** and **competence**. True, there are things in life we cannot do anything about – Covid-19 being one example – but we can choose how to deal with them.

Applying discernment allows us to **control** what we focus on so we can consciously choose the information and resources we pay attention to.

Recall from Chapter 1 that one's balloon has limited capacity for cognitive resources; we therefore need to be discerning about what resources we put into it, aiming to add resources that help our balloon RISE. As certain activities, people and thoughts can deplete our resources, causing rips in our balloon and resulting in it sinking, we must also be discerning about which activities, people and thoughts we focus on.

I remember going through a 'biker chick' phase. I had visions of being dressed in leather and a helmet, looking like Keira Knightley in that perfume advert. It turns out that the protective padding in motorcycle leathers (which was absent in the advert) makes you look like you are wearing a Captain America suit two sizes too big. When learning to ride a bike, you are taught to look to where you want to go. Sounds obvious, but I had to learn it the hard way when I lost control of the bike, panicked and all I could see ahead of me was the kerb on the opposite side of the road. Sure enough, the bike veered across the road, only stopping when it hit said kerb, throwing me over the handlebars and face-planting me in the mud on the other side. From Captain America to The Thing in an instant. My biking partner said, 'Why didn't you look at the road?' I don't know the answer to that, but I did from then on – and I reached the destination I focused on.

Your brain will react to what you focus on. Think about threats and fears and it will respond accordingly: stimulating cortisol and adrenaline, creating rips in your balloon and depleting your resources. If you choose to believe that your new boss will make your life difficult, they probably will. If you decide the latest organisational changes are ridiculous and will cause untold confusion and your job will become horrid, then it probably will.

Think about positive things, and the opposite will happen: you will increase your dopamine, be able to access the 'smarter' part of your brain and increase your resources. Choose to think that your boss is new and on a learning curve, doing the best they can, or that the long-term benefits of the organisational restructure will outweigh any initial teething problems. The ability to choose where you put your attention can change your entire being: the hormones that are produced, the physiological responses in the body and, consequently, your experience of events.

Being optimistic is having a belief that good things will happen.[77] It has been linked to happiness, perseverance, achievement and health.[78] Those who were optimistic were able to use problem-focused coping and positive reinterpretation in controllable situations.[79]

This is likely because their emotional limbic systems were quiet, allowing them to use the smart part of their brains. Choosing to focus on the positive things in life can help keep your balloon afloat.

ACTIVITY: OPTIMISM

One of the most popular assessments of optimism is the Life Orientation Test – Revised (LOT-R) created by Scheier, Carver & Bridges.[80] Recognising that we can be optimistic about some things and not about others, the LOT-R looks at your overall disposition towards optimism. Note: just because you are low on optimism does not mean you are a pessimist; those two things are on two separate scales, not at each end of one scale. The LOT-R assessment measures the amount of optimism you have and does not measure pessimism.

The questionnaire is in Appendix 3 and is also available from www.drsammather.com.

Bad stuff happens to everyone – sometimes undeserved and unfair bad stuff – but those who score higher on optimism were able to accept that which they could not control and move on.[81] They did not waste valuable resources on things that were out of their control, and this is where we need to be discerning. Are you going to dwell on the negative or the positive? The possible or the impossible? That which you can control, or that which you can't? You choose.

'I can't help what I think about!' I hear you cry. We have already talked about automatic thoughts and how we manage them in Chapter 6, but consider this: if feelings are simply messages from the brain, why can't we send a message back to the brain via feelings? Just as our brain can control our feelings, why can't we control our brain using feelings? It's a chicken-and-egg scenario, but because there is such a synergy between them we can use one to control the other. Let's look at how.

Discernment discipline step 1: Diminish your focus

Yes, discernment is a discipline. Because automatic thoughts are, well, automatic, and the brain is pre-programmed to pay more attention to threats than that which is safe, we need to be consciously discerning. Whenever things feel overwhelming, apply the discipline of discernment. It will allow you to observe the details of what is going on and make judgements as to where to invest your resources.

There are things in life that you can control, things you can influence, and then there are things that you can do nothing about. What these are will depend on your situation. When I was ten years old, I had little control over where we went on our family holiday. As I got older, I was able to influence it. Since leaving home, where I go is totally within my control.

Of course, whether I can travel to my chosen holiday destination given Covid-19 is out of my control, so I am not going to stress about my holiday destination this year. Although I can't do anything about situations outside my control, this doesn't mean I can't be concerned about them. I am concerned about climate change and the destruction of the rain forests, but the time and resources I spend worrying about it is limited because there is little I can do... or is there?

Circles of control and influence

When I created the diagram above depicting the circles of control and influence, I struggled to add anything to the 'out of my influence and control' area. As you can see, I put 'The Weather' and 'A Pandemic', but there was little else a person couldn't influence in some way. I put things like 'Climate change', 'What your organisation does' and 'Traffic' on the border of what one can and can't influence because I can influence those things within the areas I can control. I can't stop the US and China polluting and I can't stop logging firms cutting down the Amazon forest – these are out of my control. But I can do things within my circle of control such as recycling, driving an electric car and not buying 'fast fashion'. Similarly, for organisational decisions, my head office and the key decision makers may be on a different continent, but I can influence my boss and key stakeholders within my circle of control – and this is where I need to invest my resources.

Let's give a closer-to-home example: you have a presentation to give to senior leaders. You hate giving presentations and it's causing you anxiety and stress. As we know, being anxious and stressed may reduce your ability to perform well, but what exactly is causing the stress?

Is it the nature of the questions? Feeling unable to answer them? The people in the audience? The fear of getting the information wrong or the technology letting you down? What is out of your control? You may fear things like a power cut, but even then you could present without technology. Everything is within your influence or control, which means you can put things in place ahead of time to mitigate the fear. You can also influence your performance on the day. Make sure you eat and sleep well (see Chapter 4). If you need to travel, prepare in advance and ensure you get there on time. Finally, even for things which you feel you have no control over, you can choose your response.

Discernment discipline step 2: Determine the source

Are you going to focus on the negative, the things you can do nothing about (which make you feel bad), or are you going to better invest your limited resources in the positive and constructive (which make you feel better)?

Let's look at the fear of bad things happening, such as failing an exam, a driving test or a task at work. We can choose how we react to this fear. Firstly, the bad thing hasn't happened yet, and it's a waste of resources to worry about something that might never happen. As a teenager, I used to worry about nuclear war. I would spend nights awake stressing about who might 'hit the button' and what would happen. I even wrote dramatic poems about it, which my sister still uses to embarrass me at any opportunity. Not only was there nothing I could do about a nuclear war – it was outside my circle of influence or control – but I was worrying about something that didn't ever happen. What a waste of perfectly good resources (and sleep).

To use a golfing analogy, you don't choose the club you are going to use on the 10th fairway when you are at the 1st tee. You have to wait until you get there and then choose the best club depending on the situation – the specific lay of the ball, where the hole is and your ability to hit straight. So, deal with failure *if* it happens and not before. Until then, park that fear and use your resources in a more constructive way.

What happens if you do fail? Well, first of all, a wise person once said, 'There is no such thing as failure, only feedback'. You may be feeling down about what you are labelling a 'failure', but remember that your brain is creating sadness, anger and defensiveness to send you a message. You choose how you interpret the message.

We discussed the growth mindset and perspective of plenty in Chapter 6. Now would be a good time to apply them! Choose to look at the 'failure' as a learning experience and get back up and improve. The alternative is to let it rip your balloon and sink you into negativity and self-doubt – who wants to be there?

How do you apply the growth mindset and perspective of plenty? One way is to reflect. There are several reflection models out there, including the Gibbs Reflective Cycle,[82] Driscoll's What Model,[83] and Kolb's Experiential Learning Cycle;[84] however, I think they don't always guide the user deep enough inward.

A simple reflection process might look like the diagram below.

A simple reflection process based on the Gibbs Reflective Cycle

This is a great start, but it focuses on the behaviour.

Remember back in the Omnipurpose chapter we talked about how our behaviours are external demonstrations of our values and beliefs? This is important for reflection. Behaviours are the symptoms that are caused by beliefs and values, and therefore we can reflect on two levels. We can reflect on our behaviours, which can be useful, but to understand why we behave the way we do, we need to dig into our beliefs and values to address the source of our behaviours. The RISE reflection model has two layers: a behaviour-level reflection and a deeper reflection of our belief and values.

To use this model, we start at the top:

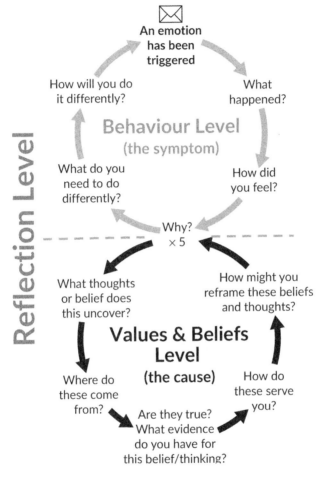

A Deeper Reflection model

An emotion has been triggered. The brain is sending you a message. If the message is sadness, anger or frustration it doesn't feel nice, so let's address it. What happened? Describe it in detail, maybe write it down. There is a guide in Appendix 4 to help you do this. Try and stick with the facts: the what, when, where and who.

Then, write down how you felt. Be specific, don't just write 'angry'. You might write, 'I felt hot, like lava was bubbling inside me', or 'I felt like crying', or 'I had a feeling in my throat' – whatever you were experiencing physically and emotionally.

Then, ask yourself why you felt like this. Then again, and again, and again, at least five times. Be careful here: you want to direct the 5 Whys inward; it's not about the other person. If you ask 'why' about the other person, firstly you will run out of steam quickly because you can't know why other people do things, you can only speculate. Secondly, other people, their reactions and their responses are outside your circle of control, and, finally, reflection's aim is learning about your reactions because those are within your circle of control. In the flowchart below, the reflection comes to an abrupt halt when the reflector decides that the boss was an idiot. Whether this is true or not is irrelevant; you can do little about that. However, if you focus the questioning on yourself and your motivations, after 5 (or more) Whys we begin to drop down into the 'behaviours and values' level of reflection. The 5 Whys have uncovered a self-doubt about the reflector's own competence.

How did you feel?

I was really angry. I felt hot and shouted. I felt like I wanted to say something mean back. So I did.

WHY?

Because my boss was unfairly accusing me of something.

Here you have a choice of direction to explore

Focus Externally on the event or other people   **Focus Internally on your feelings and responses**

WHY?

Why were you being accused?

Because my boss is an idiot and a drama queen.

WHY?		WHY?

Why are they an idiot/ drama queen?

Because they are. Who knows?

END OF PROCESS

Why did being unfairly accused make you angry?

Because I felt I had tried to do the right thing and it was being turned against me.

Why did it make you angry?

Because I wasn't being recognised for what I did do.

Cont.

WHY?

**Why do you feel the need
to be recognised?**

*Because I need to know
that people know I am
competent.*

WHY?

**Why is this important
to you?**

*Because I need the
reassurance that I am
doing a good job.*

WHY?

**Why do you need
reassurance from others?**

*Because I am not sure of
myself...*

Internal vs External Reflection

This reflection showed that what upset the person was not being unjustly accused of something, it was that the event triggered a fear (**competence**) that stemmed from a belief that they may not be a competent person, and that belief resulted in an emotional response. By changing that belief, they will change the response.

Now that the person revealed their self-belief, they can start to reflect on where it comes from. In this example, I would be asking the person: What makes you think you are not competent? Who says so? Why might they say this? What evidence do you have to a) support this view and b) discredit this view? Take a balanced approach towards this belief because you don't have to believe everything your brain tells you.

A good question to ask is, 'How does this belief serve you?' In other words, what does having this belief do for you? Does it make life better or worse? Does it add to or deplete your resources? If the answers show that the belief has a negative impact on your life, then it is a limiting belief: a belief that constrains and inhibits you. These create rips in your balloon, but you can change it by reframing it. In this example, you could reframe the belief as: 'I know sometimes I might get things wrong, but I learn from them, which increases my competence. The evidence shows that overall I am a competent person who, like everyone, sometimes gets things wrong.'

Discernment discipline step 3: Decide your response

Having reframed their belief, this person must now decide what they will do differently. They resolve to manage their automatic thoughts and remember that they are a competent person, and they decide

149

that they don't want to let one mistake define them. They now have a list of things that they want to do differently. Good.

To turn the list into a plan, this person needs to understand *how* they will do things differently. This is where they start to create new neuronal connections – a new response. At the moment, the neurons have ordered the Ego Army to defend a threat to **competence** by attacking in the form of shouting. The neurons need to create a new order for the army, and the first step is deciding what we want that order to be.

Discernment discipline step 4: Drill the new order

Let's say we don't want our Ego Armies to attack – we want them to calmly stand to attention, listen and hold their fire. We need to get the commanding neurons to change the order, and that means creating a new pathway. There are two ways to create a new pathway: practising in your head and applying it in real life.

Kolb calls the former 'abstract conceptualisation', which is a fancy way of saying 'mentally practising your response'. This starts to create a faint neuronal pathway. You can start by thinking: 'If this happened again, I would…' Replay the event with you responding in the way you want – for example, taking a deep breath and just listening to the other person. Think of this as the army being on manoeuvres. There is no real threat; it's just developing skills in case a real threat arrives.

Maybe you want to learn to walk away from a threat before you do any damage to your relationships by saying something you regret. The best way to create distance between yourself and an emotionally charged situation is to literally 'make space' and leave the situation. You can say, 'I am feeling a bit emotional / angry so I am going away to consider this. I'll call or text you when I have thought it through and am able to talk.' As long as you have communicated this calmly and responsibly, then how the other person chooses to respond is not your concern.

You may want to practise your 'escape phrase' in your head. I confess that whenever I was in a meeting where I felt my emotions rising, I would excuse myself to the bathroom. There I would practise breathing exercises (see Appendix 6) until I managed to regain control over my emotions. I was priming my army to respond differently.

Practise this new technique whenever your emotions are triggered for any reason. Each time you do, you are making the neuronal pathway stronger, the order to the Ego Army clearer. And guess what? Sometimes it might not go as planned. This will lead to an event, and an emotional reaction, and then we are right back at the top of the model, where we start again with the opportunity to continue learning about the beliefs that form our behaviours.

So far, we are being discerning about what resources we let into our balloon by focusing our attention only on that which we can control or influence, by understanding the source of our emotions and behaviours, by changing (reframing) or removing potentially negative resources, and, finally, by choosing our responses. In doing so, we are minimising the resources that could rip and deflate our balloon. I'm not saying that this will keep all negative resources away, but it will mean you have fewer to deal with.

I know this might seem like a lot of effort, and it does take time and practice. So why bother? Well, if you don't control your emotions, you will become a slave to them and how other people treat you. It will be others who determine whether your balloon is floating or sinking.

Discernment takes the power away from others and puts it in your hands – or, in this case, in your brain.

ACTIVITY

The attentional control questionnaire in Appendix 5 will help you understand how easily you can control where your attention goes.

Try improving your ability to select where you focus your attention. Meditation is a great way to do this, and it has many physical, mental and emotional benefits. Check out meditation apps such as Headspace, The Mindfulness App, Buddhify or Calm.

When feeling stressed or needing to create 'space' between an emotional event and your reaction, give breathing exercises a go. There is a sample breathing exercise for you to try in Appendix 6.

Key learnings from this chapter

- If you can't control or influence it, don't worry about it.

- If it hasn't happened yet, don't worry about it. Cross that bridge if you need to.

- The root of behaviour is our beliefs and values. Change them, and you change the behaviour.

- Learn to reflect.

- You can choose your response.

.

Conclusion

So there you have it: RISE. In order to be Resilient, have Initiative, Shift and Evolve you need to be SOUND. The SOUND person Sustains themselves so they can apply an Omnipurpose, a Useful Narrative and Discernment to the events around them.

Will this protect you from bad things happening? No; often, these are outside your circle of influence and control. But will being SOUND enable you to deal with bad things when they happen? Yes, absolutely. Having read this book, you have some tools that you can apply to enable you to maintain your resilience, take initiative, change your thinking and evolve. Are these tools easy to use? Not always. They take awareness and practice. This book has raised your awareness and shown you how to practise – the rest is up to you.

Your balloon on the RISE

In future, when you are finding things tough, you can revisit the guidance in this book and ask yourself what you could be doing differently to make your situation a little less tough. Appendix 7 has a summary of the tools we have discussed, so you have a one-page reference guide for review. After all, the only thing you truly have control over is yourself and how you choose to respond to life's situations.

Appendices

All the Appendix resources can also be found at www.drsammather.com.

Appendix 1: Your values

Identify the twelve values from the table below that are the most meaningful for you.

Accomplishment	Friendship	Ethical Standards
Integrity	Good Time/Pleasure	Nature
Community	Growth	Love
Courage	Passion	Power
Justice and Parity	Helpfulness	Recognition
Dedication	Independence	Responsibility
Money	Health (Physical/Mental)	Security
Faith	Creativity	Self-Esteem
Family	Wisdom	Spirituality

Now select your top six values and note what each means to you.

Value	For me, this means...

Appendix 2: Perspective of plenty: reflection

Think about each of these statements. Focus on your emotions. Mark the response (A or B) that best describes your emotional response:

1. You are in a meeting and several people are discussing something you know nothing about.

   A) *C**p, I have no idea what they are on about. I hope they don't find out.*

   B) *No idea what they are talking about, I'll ask them to fill me in.*

2. Your company is restructuring. They don't have a role for you in your specialism. They can offer you a role in another part of the business where you have never worked before.

   A) *I am a {insert your job function here}. It's what I do and who I am. I can't/won't do this new job.*

   B) *OK, this is new, bit concerned but I could learn a lot. I might like it.*

3. One of your team members has just upset a customer, so much so that the customer has threatened to leave/cancel an order.

   A) *Furious. That team member needs to be dealt with.*

   B) *Wow, I wonder what happened.*

4. You have messed up.

   A) *Uh oh. How can I cover this up before anyone finds out?*

   B) *I'll tell my boss what I have done and how I am going to fix it.*

5. A colleague who started with your company at the same time as you has been promoted.

   A) *Who did they sleep with?*

   B) *Good on them. I wonder what they did that I can do...*

6. An initiative you were leading has hit a setback: the senior stakeholder has changed and they are going to take some persuading.

   A) *Drat. My logic has worked once, if it doesn't work this time, there is no point arguing with idiots, I'll move on.*

   B) *My argument is not working with this person. What do I need to do differently?*

7. Your boss has given you some negative feedback that you disagree with.

   A) *S/He is an idiot. What do they know?*

   B) *Really, interesting perspective. Tell me more.*

8. Your boss sees you are tired, you have been working hard. She suggests you go home early and take a long weekend.

A) *No way, this is a trick and will be held against me. Must not show weakness.*

B) *She is right, that's a good idea.*

9. It takes a lot of effort for one of your team to complete a task.

A) *Give the task to someone who can do it more easily. Play to strengths.*

B) *How can I help this person?*

10. You have been asked to take on a new project, something you have never done before

A) *Why are they doing this? I can't do this. Why are they setting me up to fail?*

B) *OK, interesting. No idea where to start. I'll get some help.*

For the above questions, score one point for every time you selected the each 'B' answer. Add up your score and check it against the scoring table below.

Score:	0	1	2	3	4	5	6	7	8	9
		Mainly Limiting Binary Thinking				Mixed			Mainly Perspective of Plenty	

Many of you will have answered 'B' to several of the questions, giving you a high score. After all, these are the socially 'preferred' answers. But deep down

you will know some of your responses are really the
'A' ones. That's OK. We all have some elements of a
binary and limiting mindset. Go back to the questions
that you secretly know are more 'A' and consider
what your answers say about how you view various
aspects of your life.

Each of the ten questions relates to a different area and
strength. Using your score, take a look at the following table to see what it might say about your mindset.
Do you agree or disagree?

Q.	View of ...	Mainly Fixed Mind-set	Mixed	Mainly Growth Mind-set
1 ―― 2	The World	Unchangeable: find out who you are and your place in the world.	There are some areas in life where you can change but others are predetermined and no amount of effort will change them.	Changing: life is about deciding who and what you want to be and developing the skills and abilities to achieve it.
3 ―― 4	Mistakes	Hides or ignores mistakes.	We all make mistakes and they can be corrected.	See mistakes as a learning opportunity; not always about right or wrong.
5	Success of Others	Feels threatened, compares self with others, competition highlights deficits.	Selects arena of competition, will only play if convinced they will win or it will make them look good.	Looks for people to learn from; competition can improve everyone.

Continued

Cont.

Q.	View of ...	Mainly Fixed Mind-set	Mixed	Mainly Growth Mind-set
6	Difficulty/ Obstacles	Gives up.	As long as there is progress, will continue.	Keeps going because it will teach them something.
7	Feedback and Criticism	Ignores: sees feedback as a list of their faults.	Feedback can be good as long as it's relevant.	Requests both complimentary and critical feedback; it's a way to grow.
8	Offers of Help	Refuses help; it's a sign of weakness or incompetence.	Accepts help when offered.	Seeks out help; it can add to improved outcomes.
9	Effort	If I have to put this much effort in, I'm not very good.	Effort is a necessary evil. Prefers things to be easier and simple.	Effort is a path to mastery.
10	Challenge	Potential threats.	Will take on clear, immediate goals that are in areas of confidence.	Embraces this, even when can't see how to proceed.

Once you're aware of your views, consider how you might begin to change one area. Reflect on a past incident when you responded with a binary mind-set and how that felt, then replay the incident with a perspective of plenty as suggested in the table. How does that new perspective feel? It's likely to feel better, which means that if it's not adding to your resources at least it's depleting them less.

Appendix 3: Optimism questionnaire (LOT-R)[85]

Read the following sentences. For each sentence tick the box reflecting to what extent you agree or disagree with the statement.

		Strongly Disagree	Disagree	Neutral	Agree	Strongly Agree
1	In uncertain times, I usually expect the best.					
2	If something can go wrong for me, it will.					
3	I am always optimistic about my future.					
4	It's important for me to keep busy.					
5	I hardly expect things to go my way.					
6	I rarely count on good things happening to me.					
7	Overall, I expect more good things to happen to me than bad.					

For each question, circle the response you gave in the scoring table below.

Q.	Strongly Disagree	Disagree	Neutral	Agree	Strongly Agree
1	0	1	2	3	4
2	4	3	2	1	0
3	0	1	2	3	4
4	0	1	2	3	4
5	4	3	2	1	0
6	4	3	2	1	0
7	0	1	2	3	4

Now, add up the scores you circled. Where does your total score sit on the scale below?

Optimism score scale

2	4	6	8	10	12	14	16	18	20	22	24	26	28

You tend to assume the worst, believing this will prevent disappointment. But remember, this can reduce the cognitive resources in your balloon.

You look on the bright side of life, believing that things will work out in the end. This helps keep the smart part of your brain online. Be careful though: blind optimism can prevent you seeing potential risks.

Appendix 4: Reflection guide

Using the following questions as a guide, think about what happened. Describe it in detail, stick to the facts and try to be specific.

- What happened?
- When did it happen?
- Where were you?
- Who were you with?
- What were you doing?
- What were they doing?
- What did you see happen?
- What did you hear happen?
- How did you feel?
- What was happening physically?
- What thoughts were in your head?
- Describe your emotions.
- Why did you feel like this?
  - Why (×2)
  - Why (×3)
  - Why (×4)
  - Why (×5)

- What thoughts and beliefs about yourself did you uncover?

- Where do these thoughts and beliefs come from?

Now, for each belief you have identified, ask yourself the following:

- What evidence do I have to:
    - support this belief?
    - refute this belief?
- How does this belief serve you?
- How might you reframe this belief? (Choose to be kind to yourself!)
- What do you need to do differently?
- How will you change? Make an action plan.

Appendix 5: Attention questionnaire

How well can you manage your attention? For each of the questions, tick the box that applies.

		Yes, always	Mostly	Rarely	No, not at all
1	I need quiet to be able to concentrate				
2	I get distracted by what is happening around me				
3	When I feel emotional, I find it hard to concentrate				
4	I can carry on two conversations at once				
5	If I'm disturbed, I find it hard to refocus				
6	I find it easy to change my point of view				
7	When I have a long list of things to do, I find it hard to know where to start				
8	When deciding to do something, I can find myself doing something else				
9	If I am not interested in something, I find it hard to concentrate on it				

Continued

Cont.

		Yes, always	Mostly	Rarely	No, not at all
10	When I am concentrating, I am unaware of what's happening around me				
11	I usually finish one job or task before starting another				
12	I can easily move from one task to another				
13	I can block out unhelpful or irrelevant thoughts if I need to				
14	I am able to do the things I HAVE to do, even when there are things I would prefer to do				
15	I can compartmentalise things such as home and work. Emotions from one don't 'leak' into the other				
16	I am able to meditate				
17	If something upsets me, I can decide to not think about it				
18	I don't worry about that which I can't control				

Scoring

Transfer your answers to this sheet. So for question 1 if you selected 'Rarely', then circle the 2.

Q.	Yes, always	Mostly	Rarely	No, not at all
1	0	1	2	3
2	0	1	2	3
3	0	1	2	3
4	0	1	2	3
5	0	1	2	3
6	0	1	2	3
7	0	1	2	3
8	0	1	2	3
9	0	1	2	3
10	3	2	1	0
11	3	2	1	0
12	3	2	1	0
13	3	2	1	0
14	3	2	1	0
15	3	2	1	0
16	3	2	1	0
17	3	2	1	0
18	3	2	1	0

Now add up all the numbers you have circled.

Your score was between...

0-18	19-36	37-54
You find it difficult to concentrate and are easily distracted. You probably need to remove all temptations to be able to concentrate, and then only for short periods of time. That's ok, little and often is the way to go.	In some circumstances you find it difficult to concentrate and are easily distracted, but other times you are focused. Consider the conditions in which you are able to focus and create that environment when you need to concentrate.	You find it easy to focus and concentrate on the task at hand, not getting distracted by what is going on around you. This is a great skill!

You might want to explore further: Questions 1–11 assessed your ability to switch between tasks and areas of focus, while Questions 12–20 measured your ability to focus without distraction. On which set of questions did you score higher? How does this impact your daily life?

Appendix 6: Breathing exercise

This is a simple breathing exercise that you can do anywhere at any time. It can be a quick way to calm your emotions and reduce stress.

Preparation

- If you can, sit with your back straight to open up the lungs.

- Place the tip of your tongue up against the back of your front teeth.

- Exhale through your mouth and around your tongue.

Breathing steps

- Breathe out completely through your mouth, making a 'whoosh' sound.

- Close your mouth and breathe in through your nose, counting to **four** in your head.

- Hold your breath for a count of **seven**.

- Breathe out completely through your mouth, making a 'whoosh' sound, to a count of **eight**.

That is one breath. Repeat another three times.

The more you practise this, the more effective it will become at helping you quieten your emotions, relax yourself and enable clearer thinking.

Appendix 7: Toolkit summary

Your brain (Chapter 3)

Understand which '5 Cs of comfort' fear your Ego Army is reacting to:

- Cause
- Competence
- Connectedness
- Certainty
- Control

Use the SOUND principles to reflect on why and to change your response.

Being SOUND means:

Sustain (Chapter 4)

Providing your body and brain with the resources they need to maintain health and performance.

Sustain your body

- Eat (Satiate)
- Drink water (Hydrate)

- Sleep/Rest (Extricate)

- Exercise (Activate)

Sustain your brain: the 'ate' model

- Communicate

- Congregate

- Celebrate

- Educate

- Concentrate

- Create

- Decelerate

- Contemplate

- Deactivate

Omnipurpose (Chapter 5 and the Behaviour, Attitudes, Beliefs & Values model)

The overall reason for doing what you do: the meaning that makes life worth living.

Learn what your values are and begin to craft your purpose because these drive your behaviours.

Useful narrative (Chapter 6 and the Ladder of Inference)

Managing your 'inner voice' beliefs so that they become positive.

To do this, you can apply getting some perspective on things by sticking to the facts (using the ladder of influence), perspective of plenty and recognising that challenge is a way to grow outside of your comfort zone.

Discernment (Chapter 7 and Appendix 4)

Being able to recognise that we always have a choice and choosing which resources we let into our balloon.

Choose to focus only on that which is within your circle of control.

Reflect on events so that you can choose to reframe thoughts.

Dig down using the 5 Whys.

Glossary

Adrenaline Adrenaline (also known as epinephrine) and noradrenaline (also known as norepinephrine) are two related hormones that are produced in the adrenal glands (situated near the kidneys). They prepare the body for 'fight or flight' in times of stress, causing increased heart rate, heightened blood pressure, sweating and feeling shaky.

Allostasis The process that the brain uses to keep balance between stresses and coping.

Alpha waves Brain waves that operate at 8–12 Hz and occur when you are feeling relaxed.

Amygdala The part of the brain that is responsible for noticing and processing fear.

Approach vs avoid   The messages that your brain sends you in the form of emotions will tell you to approach (perception of safety) or to avoid (perception of threat).

Beta waves   Brain waves that operate at 12–35 Hz and occur when you are concentrating and problem solving.

Binary thinking   When you see the world in two dimensions: things are either good or bad, right or wrong.

Brain waves   The electrical voltages at which the brain operates.

Circle of control   Things which you can directly control and impact in your life.

Circle of influence   Things which you can't control but may be able to influence.

Cognitive processes   The mental processes in the brain: thinking, knowing, perceiving, memory, reasoning, etc.

Comfort zone   The area in which you feel comfortable executing tasks and feel competent.

Cortisol   A hormone triggered in response to threat.

Covid-19 A virus that at the time of writing has no known cure and thus forces us all to work from home and learn to use Zoom.

Delta waves Brain waves that operate at 0.5–4 Hz and occur when you are in deep sleep.

Discernment Being choosy; in this book's context, about what resources you allow into your balloon.

Dopamine A neurotransmitter that comes into play when experiencing reward/pleasure. It is also the main type of transmitter in the frontal cortex and helps control smart thinking.

Ego Army The protection that sits around our Rock of Fear. It may attack when your fears are activated or your comfort is threatened.

Emotions Also known as 'feelings'. These are messages that the brain sends you. The messages may or may not be correct.

Equilibrium That happy state when you have enough resources to be able to deal with whatever life is throwing at you.

Evolve To grow, to change, to adapt to the environment. Essential for long-term mental well-being.

Fight flight freeze The brain's automatic response to threat, triggered by the amygdala.

Frontal cortex The front part of the brain that is responsible for clever and advanced thinking.

Gamma waves Brain waves that operate at >35 Hz and occur when you are excited and highly alert.

Growth mindset A concept from Carol Dweck that reframes thinking so that experiences become a learning opportunity, allowing one to grow and improve.

Hippocampus The part of the brain involved in emotions, learning and memories.

Hypothalamus The command centre of our emotional responses, particularly to fear and threat. It activates adrenaline for fight or flight.

Ikigai The concept of finding purpose in life, making life worth living.

Imposter Syndrome A self-belief that you are not as competent or capable as others believe you to be.

Initiative The principle of being creative, proactive and applying smart thinking to new situations.

'It's only snow, get out there girls', Miss My old gym teacher who used to make us play hockey in the snow wearing stupid little skirts and short sleeved shirts. Meanwhile, she stood on the sidelines in ski wear. Someone who told me I was no good at sport.

Journey Clichéd term used by reality TV contestants and authors of self-help books. In the context of this book, it refers to learning gained from life's ups and downs.

Judgement Decisions and conclusions made about events, people or selves. They are not always correct.

Keira Knightley Actress famed for her role as Elizabeth Swan in the Pirates of the Caribbean movies and who looks amazing in the most unsafe motorcycle gear ever.

Kerb Edge of the road that proves what you focus on is where you will go.

Limbic system A term used to refer to the multiple parts of the brain that control our emotional responses.

Myelin The fatty insulation that surrounds a neuron.

Narrative The story you tell yourself. Sometimes it's fiction; sometimes it's not. Can be useful or not.

Negaton A negatively charged electron, or an attack on your happiness in the form of an insult or abuse.

Neuron A nerve cell in the brain that transmits information in the form of electrical impulses.

Neuronal path A group of connected neurons linking multiple parts of the brain together.

Omnipurpose The reason for doing what you are doing: your direction or aim in life.

Optimism A belief that good things will happen.

Peripheral processing Processing information and events using the emotional/limbic system.

Perspective of plenty The ability to see things from more than one perspective, generating multiple options and allowing you a greater choice of response.

Reflection Looking back over events and learning about yourself from them.

Reframe To position a thought or view in another way to reduce its negative impact.

Resilience   Having sufficient resources to deal with life's challenges. Similar to Equilibrium.

Resources   'Stuff' that goes into your brain: information, thoughts, food, water, social media. They can be helpful or unhelpful.

RISE   What you will do when your balloon is full of helpful resources: be Resilient, have Initiative, Switch thinking and Evolve.

Rock of Fear   The combinations of fears that may weigh down your balloon and sap your resources.

Serotonin   A neurotransmitter that stimulates 'feel good' hormones.

Shift   The ability to see things from a different view and change opinions; to respond in a different way.

Stress   The response to pressure on our resources.

Sustenance   Nutrients and behaviours that 'feed' our body and brain.

Synapse   A connection between two neurons where a chemical process takes place.

Systemic or central processing   Processing of events or situations using the smart part of the brain.

Take That   A pop group that originally had five people, then four and now three. But they write great songs.

Theta   Brain waves that operate at 4–8 Hz and occur when you are in a state of reduced consciousness but not asleep. These can lead to bursts of gamma waves when you hit upon a brilliant idea or solution.

Values   The rules by which you live your life.

Vegan   An increasingly popular dietary lifestyle that excludes any animal product. Alternative 'fake' animal products are available, and you get used to their weird taste.

Wheel of life   A tool to help you evaluate your life and what you want to focus on.

Williams, Robbie   A pop star extraordinaire. Entertainer. Ex-naughty boy, now a good bloke. Writer of hits such as 'Feel', 'Angels', 'Let Me Entertain You' and my particular favourite: 'Love My Life'. The husband I should have had.

Notes

1. Cambridge Dictionary, https://dictionary. cambridge.org/dictionary/english/sound, accessed February 2021
2. Masten et al., Resilience and development, p426
3. Bonanno, Loss, trauma, and human resilience; Glantz & Sloboda, Reconceptualization of Resilience; Luthar et al., The Construct of Resilience; Masten, Ordinary magic; McEwen, In pursuit of resilience; Staudinger et al., Reserve Capacity in Later Adulthood; Wagnild & Young, Resilience Scale; Petty & Briñol, Emotion and persuasion; Cacioppo et al., The neuroscience of persuasion

4. Wheeler et al., Resistance to persuasion as self-regulation; Maslach, *Burnout*, p5; Atouba & Lammers, Burnout among IT professionals; Maslach et al., Job burnout; Aspinwall et al., Understanding how optimism works; Baumeister et al., The strength model of self-control; Cozzarelli, Coping with abortion; Judge et al., Core self-evaluations; Kobasa, Stressful Life Events, Personality, and Health; Maier & Seligman, Learned helplessness; Taylor, Adjustment to Threatening Events

5. Population Reference Bureau, www.prb.org, accessed February 2021

6. Britt et al., Employee Resilience; Gordon & Coscarelli, Recognizing and fostering resilience; Kumpfer, Factors and processes contributing to resilience; Meredith et al., Resilience in the U.S. Military; Park, Implications of posttraumatic growth for individuals; Ryff & Singer, Flourishing under fire; Sommer, Keeping Positive and Building Strength; Sutcliffe & Vogus, Organizing for resilience

7. Marois & Ivanoff, Information Processing in the Brain

8. Baumeister et al., Ego depletion; Muraven & Baumeister, Self-regulation and depletion of limited resources; Muraven et al., Conserving Self-Control Strength

9. Job et al., Ego depletion

10. Job et al., Ego depletion
11. Baumeister et al., Personal accounts of changes in self-esteem; Hobfoll, Social and psychological resources and adaptation; Holahan et al., Resource loss, resource gain, and depressive symptoms; Keinan et al., Suppression of erroneous competing responses; King et al., Posttraumatic stress disorder in Vietnam veterans; Norris & Kaniasty, Social support in times of stress
12. McEwen, Plasticity of the Hippocampus; McEwen, In pursuit of resilience
13. Arnsten et al., The effects of stress exposure on prefrontal cortex; Compas, Psychobiological processes of stress and coping; Kalisch et al., Deconstructing and reconstructing resilience; McEwen & Sapolsky, Stress and Cognitive Function
14. See Note 8
15. McEwen & Gianaros, The brain in stress and adaptation
16. McEwen, In pursuit of resilience
17. Hobfoll, Social and psychological resources and adaptation; Hobfoll, Conservation of Resources, p516
18. Hobfoll, Social and psychological resources and adaptation; Seligman & Csikszentmihalyi, Positive psychology

19. Albarracín & Kumkale, Affect as information in persuasion; Schwarz & Clore, Judgments of well-being
20. Bohner et al., Information Processing Approaches to Persuasion; Petty & Briñol, Emotion and persuasion; Sweldens et al., Awareness in Attitude Formation
21. Gawronski & Bodenhausen, Associative and propositional processes in evaluation
22. See Note 17
23. Petty & Briñol, Emotion and persuasion
24. Cacioppo et al., The neuroscience of persuasion; Mather, Employee Safety; Wheeler et al., Resistance to persuasion as self-regulation
25. Kumpfer, Factors and processes contributing to resilience, p180
26. Bonanno, Loss, trauma, and human resilience; Zautra & Reich, Resilience, p173; Garmezy, Resilience in Children's Adaptation; Masten, Ordinary magic
27. Bonanno, Loss, trauma, and human resilience; Masten, Ordinary magic; Glantz & Sloboda, Analysis and Reconceptualization of Resilience; Luthar et al., The Construct of Resilience; McEwen, In pursuit of resilience; Staudinger et al., Resilience in Later Adulthood; Wagnild & Young, Resilience Scale
28. Gordon, Resilient African American High School Students; Luthans, Positive organizational behavior

29. Youssef & Luthans, Positive organizational behavior in the workplace; Beltman et al., Thriving not just surviving, p186; Näswall et al., EmpRes Measurement Properties, p1; Compas, Psychobiological processes of stress and coping, p226

30. Joseph et al., Changes in outlook following disaster; Tedeschi & Calhoun, The Posttraumatic Growth Inventory; Tedeschi & Calhoun, Posttraumatic Growth

31. Bensimon, Trauma, PTSD and posttraumatic growth; Frazier et al., Self-Reported Posttraumatic Growth; Videka-Sherman, The limits of recovery

32. Park, Posttraumatic growth for individuals

33. Pargament & Park, Merely a Defense?

34. Joseph et al., Changes in outlook following disaster

35. Tedeschi & Calhoun, Posttraumatic Growth; Wortman, Posttraumatic Growth

36. Bensimon, Trauma, PTSD and posttraumatic growth; Wortman, Posttraumatic Growth; Bonanno et al., Trajectories of grieving, pp287, 307; Helgeson et al., Benefit finding and growth

37. Egeland et al., Resilience as Process

38. Zautra & Reich, Resilience, p173; Lang, The Emotion Probe; Lazarus & Folkman, Emotions and coping

39. Albarracín & Kumkale, Affect as information in persuasion; Clore & Huntsinger, How emotions inform judgment and regulate thought; Huntsinger et al., The affective control of thought

40. Zautra & Reich, Resilience, p173; Tedeschi & Calhoun, Posttraumatic Growth; Cacioppo et al., The affect system; Lang, The Emotion Probe

41. Bonanno, Resilience in the face of potential trauma; Caza and Milton, Resilience at work. In *The Oxford Handbook of Positive Organizational Scholarship*; Wortman, Posttraumatic growth: Progress and problems

42. Kumpfer, Factors and processes contributing to resilience, p180; Meredith, Sherbourne, Gaillot, Hansell, Ritschard, Parker & Wren, Promoting psychological resilience in the military; Park, Posttraumatic growth for individuals; Ryff & Singer, Flourishing under fire: Resilience as a prototype of challenged thriving; Sommer, Keeping Positive and Building Strength: The Role of Affect and Team Leadership in Developing Resilience During an Organizational Crisis; Sutcliffe & Vogus, Organizing for Resilience

43. Kahn, W. A. (1990). Psychological Conditions of Personal Engagement and Disengagement at Work. *Academy of Management Journal*, 33(4), 692–724. doi:10.2307/256287; Luthans, F., Avey, J. B., Avolio, B. J., & Peterson, S. J. (2010). The Development and Resulting Performance Impact of Positive Psychological Capital. *Human Resource Development Quarterly*, 21(1), 41–67. doi:10.1002/hrdq.20034; Pearlin, L. I., & Schooler, C. (1978). Structure of Coping. *Journal of Health and Social Behavior*, 19(1), 2–21. doi: 10.2307/2136319;

Van den Heuvel, M., Demerouti, E., Bakker, A. B., Schaufeli, W. B., Houdmont, J., & Leka, S. (2010). Personal resources and work engagement in the face of change. *Contemporary Occupational Health Psychology: Global Perspectives on Research and Practice*, 1, 124–150

44. Bennett, N., & Lemoine, G. J. (2014a). What a difference a word makes: Understanding threats to performance in a VUCA world. *Business Horizons*, 57(3), 311–317, p27

45. Lamberson, Breaking the connection between stress and tunnel vision; Dirkin, Cognitive Tunneling: Use of Visual Information under Stress

46. Perez-Valenzuela & Terreros, Effects of stress on the auditory system: An approach to study a common origin for mood disorders and dementia; Aboitiz & Dagnino-Subiabre, Stress effects on the auditory system and fear processing in the brain

47. Arnsten et al., 2015; Compas, 2006; Kalisch et al., 2019; McEwen, 1995 (Hohnen & Murphy, 2016; Willis, 2010)

48. Clore & Huntsinger, How emotions inform judgment and regulate thought; Ashby, Isen, & Turken, A neuropsychological theory of positive affect and its influence on cognition

49. Bakker & Demerouti, The job demands-resources model: State of the art; Hobfoll, Social and psychological resources and adaptation

50. Albarracín & Kumkale, Affect as information in persuasion; Clore & Huntsinger, How emotions inform judgment and regulate thought; Huntsinger et al., The affective control of thought
51. Kahneman, K, *Thinking, Fast and Slow* (Penguin, 2012)
52. Johnson, S, *Who Moved My Cheese?*
53. Beechler & Woodward, The Global War for Talent; Weick & Quinn, Organisational Change and Development; Worrall & Cooper, The Quality of Working Life, Managers Wellbeing, Motivation and Productivity
54. Beechler & Woodward, The Global War for Talent; McArthur, Beating VUCA's Whiplash Factor
55. McArthur, Beating VUCA's Whiplash Factor
56. Aspinwall et al., Understanding how optimism works; Chung et al., Resistance to organizational change
57. Bruggeman et al., Effects of Excessive Fructose
58. Armstrong et al., Mild dehydration affects mood; Ganio et al., Mild dehydration impairs cognitive performance; Kempton et al., Dehydration affects brain structure and function; Lindseth et al., Effects of hydration on cognitive function of pilots
59. Li et al., REM sleep
60. Craft & Perna, The Benefits of Exercise for the Clinically Depressed
61. Grisel et al., Influence of beta-Endorphin on anxious behavior in mice

62. Zorrilla et al., Basal pituitary-adrenal hormone levels

63. Alty et al., Exercise and dementia prevention

64. Bullock & Giesbrecht, Acute exercise and aerobic fitness influence selective attention; Sanders et al., Exercise and cognitive function in older adults; Sáez de Asteasu et al., Impact of physical exercise on cognitive function in older medical patients

65. Okano, S., & Takeuchi, K. (2017). The Effects of Japanese Shingon Esoteric Buddhism Meditation on Human Stress Management. *Journal of the Institute of Industrial Applications Engineers*, 5(1), 37, https://doi.org/10.12792/jiiae.5.37

66. Judge et al., Core self-evaluations and job and life satisfaction

67. Ryan et al., Self-Complexity and the Authenticity of Self-Aspects

68. Rothmann & Welsh, Employee engagement

69. Creswell et al., Affirmation of Personal Values

70. Higgins et al., Self and Health

71. Kwon, More women like me are choosing to be childfree

72. Sone et al., Sense of life worth living (ikigai) and mortality in Japan

73. Mather, S. A. (2020). The Contribution of Psychological Resources in the Creation of Employee Psychological Safety (Doctoral dissertation, University of Reading), http://centaur.reading.ac.uk/95651/

74. Mitsuhashi, *Ikigai: Giving every day meaning and joy*

75. Dweck, What having a 'growth mindset' actually means

76. https://www.dictionary.com, accessed February 2021

77. Fibel & Hale, The Generalized Expectancy for Success Scale: A new measure; Schier & Carver, Optimism, Coping, and Health - Assessment and Implications of Generalized Outcome Expectancies; Rotter, Generalized expectancies for internal versus external control of reinforcement

78. Cozzarelli, Personality and self-efficacy as predictors of coping with abortion; Fibel & Hale, The Generalized Expectancy for Success Scale: A new measure; Mulkhana & Hailey, The role of optimism in health-enhancing behavior; Peterson, The future of optimism; Scheier & Carver, Optimism, Coping, and Health - Assessment and Implications of Generalized Outcome Expectancies; Segerstrom, Taylor & Kemeny, Optimism is associated with mood, coping, and immune change in response to stress; Seligman, Building Human Strength: Psychology's Forgotten Mission; Snyder, Sympson, Michael & Cheavens, Optimism and hope constructs: Variants on a positive expectancy theme; Taylor, Kemeny, Reed, Bower & Gruenewald, Psychological resources,

positive illusions, and health; Tiger, *Optimism: The biology of hope*

79. Scheier, M. F., Weintraub, J. K., & Carver, C. S. (1986). Coping with stress: Divergent strategies of optimists and pessimists. *Journal of Personality and Social Psychology, 51*(6), 1257–1264. doi:10.1037/0022-3514.51.6.1257

80. Scheier et al., Distinguishing optimism from neuroticism

81. Scheier et al., Distinguishing optimism from neuroticism; Lazarus & Folkman, Transactional theory and research on emotions and coping

82. Gibbs, *Learning by Doing*

83. Driscoll, *Practising Clinical Supervision*

84. Kolb, *Experiential Learning*

85. Scheier et al., Distinguishing optimism from neuroticism

References

Albarracín, D., & Kumkale, G. T. (2003). Affect as information in persuasion: A model of affect identification and discounting. *Journal of Personality and Social Psychology*, 84(3), 453-469. doi: 10.1037/0022-3514. 84.3.453.

Alty J., Farrow M., & Lawler, K. (2020). Exercise and dementia prevention. *Practical Neurology*, 20, 234–240.

Armstrong, L. E., Ganio, M. S., Casa, D. J., Lee, E. C., McDermott, B. P., Klau, J. F., Jimenez, L., Le Bellego, L., Chevillotte, E., & Lieberman, H. R. (2012). Mild dehydration affects mood in healthy young women. *The Journal of Nutrition*, 142(2), 382–388.

Arnsten, A. F. T., Raskind, M. A., Taylor, F. B., & Connor, D. F. (2015). The effects of stress exposure on prefrontal cortex: Translating basic research into successful treatments for post-traumatic stress disorder. *Neurobiology of Stress*, 1, 10. doi: http://dx.doi.org/10.1016/j.ynstr.2014.10.002.

Aspinwall, L. G., Richter, L., & Hoffman, R. (2001). Understanding how optimism works: An examination of optimists' adaptive moderation of belief and behavior. In E. C. Chang (Ed.), *Optimism and pessimism: Implications for theory, research, and practice*, 217–238. Washington, D.C.: American Psychological Association.

Atouba, Y. C., & Lammers, J. C. (2018). Examining the relationships between participative organisational communication practices and burnout among IT professionals. *Total Quality Management & Business Excellence*, 31(7–8), 1–15.

Baumeister, R. F., Dori, G. A., & Hastings, S. (1998). Belongingness and temporal bracketing in personal accounts of changes in self-esteem. *Journal of Research in Personality*, 32(2), 222–235. doi: 10.1006/jrpe.1998.2218.

Baumeister, R. F., Muraven, M., & Tice, D. M. (2000). Ego depletion: A resource model of volition, self-regulation, and controlled processing. *Social Cognition*, 18(2), 130–150. doi: 10.1521/soco.2000.18.2.130.

Baumeister, R. F., Vohs, K. D., & Tice, D. M. (2007). The strength model of self-control. *Current Directions in Psychological Science*, 16(6), 351–355.

Beltman, S., Mansfield, C., & Price, A. (2011). Thriving not just surviving: A review of research on teacher resilience. *Educational Research Review*, 6(3), 186. doi: 10.1016/j.edurev.2011.09.001.

Bensimon, M. (2012). Elaboration on the association between trauma, PTSD and posttraumatic growth: The role of trait resilience. *Personality and Individual Differences*, 52(7), 782–787. doi: 10.1016/j.paid.2012.01.011.

Bohner, G., Erb, H.-P., & Siebler, F. (2008). Information Processing Approaches to Persuasion: Integrating Assumptions from the Dual- and Single-Processing Perspectives. In W. D. Crano & R. Prislin (Eds.), *Attitudes and attitude change*, 161–189. New York: Taylor and Francis.

Bonanno, G. A. (2004). Loss, trauma, and human resilience – Have we underestimated the human capacity to thrive after extremely aversive events? *American Psychologist*, 59(1), 20–28. doi: 10.1037/0003-066x.59.1.20.

Bonanno, G. A., Boerner, K., & Wortman, C. B. (2008). Trajectories of grieving. *Handbook of Bereavement Research and Practice: Advances in Theory and Intervention*, 287–307. Cambridge University Press, UK.

Britt, T. W., Shen, W., Sinclair, R. R., Grossman, M. R., & Klieger, D. M. (2016). How Much Do We Really Know About Employee Resilience? *Industrial and Organizational Psychology*, 9(02), 378–404. doi: 10.1017/iop.2015.107.

Bruggeman, E. C., Ross, A. P. & Parent, M. B. (2012). Detrimental Effects of Excessive Fructose Ingestion on Memory and other Brain Functions. In Johnston & Collins (Eds.). *Fructose*, 81–100. Nova Science Publisher, New York.

Bullock, T., & Giesbrecht, B. (2014). Acute exercise and aerobic fitness influence selective attention during visual search. *Frontiers in Psychology*, 5, 1290.

Cacioppo, J. T., Cacioppo, S., & Petty, R. E. (2018). The neuroscience of persuasion: A review with an emphasis on issues and opportunities. *Social Neuroscience*, 13(2), 129–172. doi: 10.1080/17470919.2016.1273851.

Cacioppo, J. T., Gardner, W. L., & Berntson, G. G. (1999). The affect system has parallel and integrative processing components: Form follows function. *Journal of Personality and Social Psychology*, 76(5), 839–855. doi: 10.1037/0022-3514.76.5.839.

Carver, C. S., & Scheier, M. F. (1990). Origins and Functions of Positive and Negative Affect – a Control-Process View. *Psychological Review*, 97(1), 19–35. doi: 10.1037/0033-295x.97.1.19.

Carver, C. S., & Scheier, M. F. (2002). The hopeful optimist. *Psychological Inquiry*, 13(4), 288–290.

Chung, S.-H., Su, Y.-F., & Su, S.-W. (2012). The impact of cognitive flexibility on resistance to organizational change. *Social Behavior and Personality: an international journal*, 40(5), 735–745.

Clore, G. L., & Huntsinger, J. R. (2007). How emotions inform judgment and regulate thought. *Trends in Cognitive Sciences*, 11(9), 393-399. doi: 10.1016/j.tics.2007.08.005.

Compas, B. E. (2006). Psychobiological processes of stress and coping – Implications for resilience in children and adolescents – Comments on the papers of Romeo & McEwen and Fisher et al.

Resilience in Children, 1094(1), 226–234. doi: 10.1196/annals.1376.024.

Cozzarelli, C. (1993). Personality and self-efficacy as predictors of coping with abortion. *Journal of Personality and Social Psychology*, 65(6), 1224–1236. doi: 10.1037/0022-3514.65.6.1224.

Craft, L. L., & Perna, F. M. (2004). The Benefits of Exercise for the Clinically Depressed. *Primary Care Companion to the Journal of Clinical Psychiatry*, 6(3), 104–111. https://doi.org/10.4088/pcc.v06n0301.

Creswell, J. D., Welch, W. T., Taylor, S. E., Sherman, D. K., Gruenewald, T. L., & Mann, T. (2005). Affirmation of Personal Values Buffers Neuroendocrine and Psychological Stress Responses. *Psychological Science*, 16(11), 846–851. doi: 10.1111/j.1467-9280.2005.01624.x.

Derryberry, D., & Reed, M., A. (2002). Anxiety-related attentional biases and their regulation by attentional control. *Journal of Abnormal Psychology*, 111(2), 225–236. doi: 10.1037/0021-843X.111.2.225.

Driscoll, J. (Ed.). (2007). *Practising Clinical Supervision: A Reflective Approach for Healthcare Professionals.* Edinburgh: Elsevier.

Dweck, C. (2016). What having a 'growth mindset' actually means. *Harvard Business Review*, 13.

Egeland, B., Carlson, E., & Sroufe, L. A. (1993). Resilience as Process. *Development and Psychopathology*, 5(4), 517–528.

Eiseley, L, *The Star Thrower* (1979, Harcourt Publishers Ltd).

Fay, D., & Frese, M. (2001). The concept of personal initiative: An overview of validity studies. *Human Performance*, 14(1), 97–124.

Frazier, P., Tennen, H., Gavian, M., Park, C., Tomich, P., & Tashiro, T. (2009). Does Self-Reported Posttraumatic Growth Reflect Genuine Positive Change? *Psychological Science*, 20(7), 912–919.

Frese, M., & Fay, D. (2001). 4. Personal initiative: An active performance concept for work in the 21st century. *Research in Organizational Behavior*, 23, 133–187.

Ganio, M. S., Armstrong, L. E., Casa, D. J., McDermott, B. P., Lee, E. C., Yamamoto, L. M., Marzano, S., Lopez, R. M., Jimenez, L., Le Bellego, L., Chevillotte, E., & Lieberman, H. R. (2011). 'Mild dehydration impairs cognitive performance and mood of men', *British Journal of Nutrition*, 106(10), 1535–1543.

Garmezy, N. (1991). Resilience in Children's Adaptation to Negative Life Events and Stressed Environments. *Pediatric Annals*, 20(9), 459–466.

Gawronski, B., & Bodenhausen, G. V. (2006). Associative and propositional processes in evaluation: An integrative review of implicit and explicit attitude change. *Psychological Bulletin*, 132(5), 692–731. doi: 10.1037/0033-2909.132.5.692.

Gibbs, G. (1998). *Learning by Doing: A guide to teaching and learning methods*. Oxford: Further Education Unit, Oxford Polytechnic.

Glantz, M. D., & Sloboda, Z. (2002). Analysis and Reconceptualization of Resilience. In M. D. Glantz

& J. L. Johnson (Eds.), *Resilience and Development: Positive Life Adaptations*, 109–126. Boston, MA: Springer US.

Gordon, K. A. (1995). Self-Concept and Motivational Patterns of Resilient African American High School Students. *Journal of Black Psychology*, 21(3), 239–255. doi: 10.1177/00957984950213003.

Gordon, K. A., & Coscarelli, W. C. (1996). Recognizing and fostering resilience. *Performance Improvement*, 35(9), 14–17.

Grisel J. E., Bartels J. L., Allen S. A., & Turgeon V. L. (2008). Influence of beta-Endorphin on anxious behavior in mice: interaction with EtOH. *Psychopharmacology (Berl)*, 200(1), 105–115. doi: 10.1007/s00213-008-1161-4.

Helgeson, V. S., Reynolds, K. A., & Tomich, P. L. (2006). A meta-analytic review of benefit finding and growth. *Journal of Consulting and Clinical Psychology*, 74(5), 797–816. doi: 10.1037/0022-006X.74.5.797.

Higgins, E. T., Vookles, J., & Tykocinski, O. (1992). Self and Health: How 'Patterns' of Self-Beliefs Predict Types of Emotional and Physical Problems. *Social Cognition*, 10(1), 25. doi: 10.1521/soco.1992.10.1.125.

Hobfoll, S. E. (1989). Conservation of Resources – a New Attempt at Conceptualizing Stress. *American Psychologist*, 44(3), 513–524. doi: 10.1037/0003-066x.44.3.513.

Hobfoll, S. E. (2002). Social and psychological resources and adaptation. *Review of General Psychology*, 6(4), 307–324. doi: 10.1037//1089-2680.6.4.307.

Holahan, C. J., Moos, R. H., Holahan, C. K., & Cronkite, R. C. (1999). Resource loss, resource gain, and depressive symptoms: A 10-year model. *Journal of Personality and Social Psychology*, 77(3), 620–629. doi: 10.1037/0022-3514.77.3.620.

Huntsinger, J. R., Isbell, L. M., & Clore, G. L. (2014). The affective control of thought: Malleable, not fixed. *Psychological Review*, 121(4), 600–618. doi: 10.1037/a0037669.

Job, V., Dweck, C. S., & Walton, G. M. (2010). Ego depletion – is it all in your head? Implicit theories about willpower affect self-regulation. *Psychological Science*, 21(11), 1686–1693. doi: 10.1177/0956797610384745.

Joseph, S., Williams, R., & Yule, W. (1993). Changes in outlook following disaster: The preliminary development of a measure to assess positive and negative responses. *Journal of Traumatic Stress*, 6(2), 271–279. doi: 10.1002/jts.2490060209.

Judge, T. A., Bono, J. E., Erez, A., & Locke, E. A. (2005). Core self-evaluations and job and life satisfaction: The role of self-concordance and goal attainment. *Journal of Applied Psychology*, 90(2), 257–268. doi: 10.1037/0021-9010.90.2.257.

Kalisch, R., Cramer, A. O., Binder, H., Fritz, J., Leertouwer, I., Lunansky, G., Meyer, B., Timmer, J., Veer, I. M., Van Harmelen, A.-L. (2019). Deconstructing and reconstructing resilience: a dynamic network approach. *Perspectives on Psychological Science*, 14(5), 765–777.

Keinan, G., Friedland, N., Kahneman, D., & Roth, D. (1999). The effect of stress on the suppression of erroneous competing responses. *Anxiety, Stress & Coping*, 12(4), 455–476.

Kempton, M. J., Ettinger, U., Foster, R., Williams, S. R., Calvert, G. A., Hampshire, A., Zelaya, F. O., O'Gorman, R. L., McMorris, T., Owen, A. M., & Smith, M. S. (2011). Dehydration affects brain structure and function in healthy adolescents. *Human Brain Mapping*, 32(1), 71–79.

King, D. W., King, L. A., Foy, D. W., Keane, T. M., & Fairbank, J. A. (1999). Posttraumatic stress disorder in a national sample of female and male Vietnam veterans. Risk factors, war-zone stressors, and resilience-recovery variables. *Journal of Abnormal Psychology*, 108(1), 164–170. doi: 10.1037/0021-843x.108.1.164.

Kobasa, S. C. (1979). Stressful Life Events, Personality, and Health – Inquiry into Hardiness. *Journal of Personality and Social Psychology*, 37(1), 1–11. doi: 10.1037/0022-3514.37.1.1.

Kolb, D. (1984). *Experiential Learning: Experience as the source of learning and development.* Upper Saddle River, NJ: Prentice Hall.

Kumpfer, K. L. (2002). Factors and processes contributing to resilience. In *Resilience and Development*, 179–224. Springer. Boston, MA.

Kwon, R. O. More women like me are choosing to be childfree. Is this the age of opting out? *The Guardian*, 6th July 2020.

Lang, P. J. (1995). The Emotion Probe – Studies of Motivation and Attention. *American Psychologist*, 50(5), 372–385. doi: 10.1037//0003-066x.50.5.372.

Lazarus, R. S., & Folkman, S. (1987). Transactional theory and research on emotions and coping. *European Journal of Personality*, 1(3), 141–169. doi: 10.1002/per.2410010304.

Li, W., Ma, L., Yang, G., & Gan, W. B. (2017). REM sleep selectively prunes and maintains new synapses in development and learning. *Nature Neuroscience*, 20(3), 427–437.

Lindseth, P. D., Lindseth, G. N., Petros, T. V., Jensen, W. C., & Caspers, J. (2013). Effects of hydration on cognitive function of pilots. *Military Medicine*, 178(7), 792–798.

Luthans, F. (2002). Positive organizational behavior: Developing and managing psychological strengths. *Academy of Management Executive*, 16(1).

Luthar, S. S., Cicchetti, D., & Becker, B. (2000). The Construct of Resilience: A Critical Evaluation and Guidelines for Future Work. *Child Development*, 71(3), 543–562. doi: 10.1111/1467-8624.00164.

Maier, S. F., & Seligman, M. E. P. (1976). Learned helplessness: Theory and evidence. *Journal of Experimental Psychology. General*, 105(1), 3–46. doi: 10.1037/0096-3445.105.1.3.

Marois, R. & Ivanoff, J. (2005). Capacity Limits of Information Processing in the Brain. *Trends in Cognitive Sciences*, 9(6), 296–305.

Maslach, C. (2003). *Burnout: The Cost of Caring*, 5. Cambridge, MA: Malor Books.

Maslach, C., Schaufeli, W. B., & Leiter, M. P. (2001). Job burnout. *Annual Review of Psychology*, 52, 397–422. doi: 10.1146/annurev.psych.52.1.397.

Masten, A. S. (2001). Ordinary magic – Resilience processes in development. *American Psychologist*, 56(3), 227–238. doi: 10.1037//0003-066x.56.3.227.

Masten, A. S., Best, K. M., & Garmezy, N. (1990). Resilience and development: Contributions from the study of children who overcome adversity. *Development and Psychopathology*, 2(4), 426.

Mather, S. (2020). The Contribution of Psychological Resources in the Creation of Employee Safety. (PhD thesis), University of Reading, England.

McEwen, B. S. (2001). Plasticity of the Hippocampus: Adaptation to Chronic Stress and Allostatic Load. *Annals of the New York Academy of Sciences*, 933(1), 265–277. doi: 10.1111/j.1749-6632.2001.tb05830.x.

McEwen, B. S. (2016). In pursuit of resilience: stress, epigenetics, and brain plasticity. *Annals of the New York Academy of Sciences*, 1373(1), 56–64. doi:10.1111/nyas.13020.

McEwen, B. S., & Gianaros, P. J. (2010). Central role of the brain in stress and adaptation: Links to socio-economic status, health, and disease. *Biology of Disadvantage: Socioeconomic Status and Health*, 1186, 190–222. doi: 10.1111/j.1749- 6632.2009.05331.x.

McEwen, B. S., & Sapolsky, R. M. (1995). Stress and Cognitive Function. *Current Opinion in Neurobiology*, 5(2), 205–216.

Meredith, L. S., Sherbourne, C. D., Gaillot, S. J., Hansell, L., Ritschard, H. V., Parker, A. M., & Wrenn, G.

(2011). Promoting Psychological Resilience in the U.S. Military. *Rand Health Quarterly*, 1(2), 2.

Mitsuhashi, Y. (2018). *Ikigai: Giving every day meaning and joy*. Kyle Books, Hachette, UK.

Muraven, M., & Baumeister, F. (2000). Self-regulation and depletion of limited resources: Does self-control resemble a muscle? *Psychological Bulletin*, 126(2), 247–259. doi: 10.1037/0033-2909.126.2.247.

Muraven., M., Shmueli, D., & Burkley, E. (2006). Conserving Self-Control Strength. *Journal of Personality and Social Psychology*, 91(3 September 2006), 13.

Näswall, K., Kuntz, J., Hodliffe, M., & Malinen, S. (2015). *Employee Resilience Scale (EmpRes) Measurement Properties*. Resilient Organisations Ltd, Christchurch, New Zealand.

Norris, F. H., & Kaniasty, K. (1996). Received and perceived social support in times of stress: A test of the social support deterioration deterrence model. *Journal of Personality and Social Psychology*, 71(3), 498–511. doi: 10.1037/0022- 3514.71.3.498.

Pargament, K. I., & Park, C. L. (1995). Merely a Defense? The Variety of Religious Means and Ends. *Journal of Social Issues*, 51(2), 13–32. doi: 10.1111/j.1540-4560.1995.tb01321.x.

Park, C. L. (1998). Implications of posttraumatic growth for individuals. In *Posttraumatic Growth: Positive Changes in the Aftermath of Crisis*, 153–177. Tedeschi, Park & Calhoun (Eds). Lawrence Erlbaum Associates, London.

Peterson, C. (2000). The future of optimism. *American Psychologist*, 55(1), 44–55. doi: 10.1037//0003-066x.55.1.44.

Petty, R. E., & Briñol, P. (2015). Emotion and persuasion: Cognitive and meta-cognitive processes impact attitudes. *Cognition and Emotion*, 29(1), 1–26. doi: 10.1080/02699931.2014.967183.

Rini, C. K., Dunkel-Schetter, C., Wadhwa, P. D., & Sandman, C. A. (1999). Psychological adaptation and birth outcomes: The role of personal resources, stress, and sociocultural context in pregnancy. *Health Psychology*, 18(4), 333–345. doi: 10.1037/0278-6133.18.4.333.

Rothmann, S., & Welsh, C. (2013). Employee engagement: The role of psychological conditions. *Management Dynamics: Journal of the Southern African Institute for Management Scientists*, 22(1), 14–25.

Ryan, R. M., LaGuardia, J. G., & Rawsthorne, L. J. (2005). Self-Complexity and the Authenticity of Self-Aspects: Effects on Well Being and Resilience to Stressful Events. *North American Journal of Psychology*, 7(3), 431–447.

Ryff, C. D., & Singer, B. (2003). Flourishing under fire: Resilience as a prototype of challenged thriving. In *Flourishing: Positive Psychology and the Life Well-Lived*, 15–36. American Psychological Association, Washington, D.C.

Sáez de Asteasu, M. L., Martínez-Velilla, N., Zambom-Ferraresi, F., Casas-Herrero, Á., Cadore, E. L., Galbete, A., & Izquierdo, M. (2019). Assessing the impact of physical exercise on cognitive function in older medical patients during acute hospitalization: Secondary analysis of a random-ized trial. *PLoS Medicine*, 16(7), e1002852.

Sanders, L. M., Hortobágyi, T., la Bastide-van Gemert, S., van der Zee, E. A., & van Heuvelen, M. J. (2019). Dose-response relationship between exercise and cognitive function in older adults with and with-out cognitive impairment: a systematic review and meta-analysis. *PLoS One*, 14(1), e0210036.

Scheier, M. F., & Carver, C. S. (1985). Optimism, Coping, and Health – Assessment and Implica-tions of Generalized Outcome Expectancies. *Health Psychology*, 4(3), 219–247. doi: 10.1037//0278-6133.4.3.219.

Scheier, M. F., Carver, C. S., & Bridges M. W. (1994). Distinguishing optimism from neuroticism (and trait anxiety, self-mastery, and self-esteem): A reevaluation of the Life Orientation Test. *Journal of Personality and Social Psychology*, 67(6), 1063–1078. doi: 10.1037/0022-3514.67.6.1063.

Schwarz, N., & Clore, G. L. (1983). Mood, misattri-bution, and judgments of well-being: Informative and directive functions of affective states. *Journal of Personality and Social Psychology*, 45(3), 513–523. doi: 10.1037/0022-3514.45.3.513.

Segerstrom, S. C., Taylor, S. E., Kemeny, M. E., & Fahey, J. L. (1998). Optimism is associated with mood, coping, and immune change in response to stress. *Journal of Personality and Social Psychology*, 74(6), 1646–1655. doi: 10.1037/0022-3514.74.6.1646.

Seligman, M. E., & Csikszentmihalyi, M. (2000). Positive psychology: An introduction. *American Psychologist*, 55(1), 5–14.

Senge, P. M. (1990) The Fifth Discipline: The art and practice of the learning organization. New York: Doubleday/Currency.

Snyder, C. R., Sympson, S. C., Michael, S. T., & Cheavens, J. (2001). Optimism and hope constructs: Variants on a positive expectancy theme. In *Optimism and Pessimism: Implications for Theory, Research, and Practice*, 101–125. Chang, E. (Ed). American Psychological Association, Washington, D.C.

Sommer, S. A. (2016). Keeping Positive and Building Strength: The Role of Affect and Team Leadership in Developing Resilience During an Organizational Crisis. *Group & Organization Management*, 41(2), 172–202. doi: 10.1177/1059601115578027.

Sone, T., Nakaya, N., Ohmori, K., Shimazu, T., Higashiguchi, M., Kakizaki, M., Nobutaka, K., Kuriyama, S., & Tsuji, I., (2008). Sense of life worth living (ikigai) and mortality in Japan: Ohsaki Study. *Psychosomatic Medicine*, 70(6), 709–715.

Staudinger, U. M., Marsiske, M., & Baltes, P. B. (1993). Resilience and Levels of Reserve Capacity in Later Adulthood – Perspectives from Life-Span Theory. *Development and Psychopathology*, 5(4), 541–566.

Sutcliffe, K. M., & Vogus, T. J. (2003). Organizing for resilience. In *Positive Organizational Scholarship*, 94–110. Cameron, K. S., Dutton, J. E., and Quinn,

R. E., (Eds). Berrett-Koehler Publishers, Oakland, California.

Sweldens, S., Corneille, O., & Yzerbyt, V. (2014). The Role of Awareness in Attitude Formation Through Evaluative Conditioning. *Personality and Social Psychology Review*, 18(2), 187–209. doi: 10.1177/1088868314527832.

Taylor, S. E. (1983). Adjustment to Threatening Events – a Theory of Cognitive Adaptation. *American Psychologist*, 38(11), 1161–1173. doi: 10.1037//0003-066x.38.11.1161.

Taylor, S. E., Kemeny, M. E., Reed, G. M., Bower, J. E., & Gruenewald, T. L. (2000). Psychological resources, positive illusions, and health. *American Psychologist*, 55(1), 99–109. doi: 10.1037//0003-066x.55.1.99.

Tedeschi, R. G., & Calhoun, L. G. (1996). The Posttraumatic Growth Inventory: Measuring the positive legacy of trauma. *Journal of Traumatic Stress*, 9(3), 455–471.

Tedeschi, R. G., & Calhoun, L. G. (2004). Posttraumatic Growth: Conceptual Foundations and Empirical Evidence. *Psychological Inquiry*, 15(1), 1–18.

Videka-Sherman, L., & Lieberman, M. (1985). The effects of self-help and psychotherapy intervention on child loss: The limits of recovery. *American Journal of Orthopsychiatry*, 55(1), 70–82. doi: 10.1111/j.1939-0025.1985.tb03422.x.

Wagnild, G. M., & Young, H. M. (1993). Development and psychometric evaluation of the Resilience Scale. *Journal of Nursing Measurement*, 1(2), 165–178.

Wheeler, S. C., Briñol, P., & Hermann, A. D. (2007). Resistance to persuasion as self-regulation: Ego-depletion and its effects on attitude change processes. *Journal of Experimental Social Psychology*, 43(1), 150–156. doi: 10.1016/j.jesp.2006.01.001.

Wortman, C. B. (2004). Posttraumatic growth: Progress and problems. *Psychological Inquiry*, 15(1), 81–90.

Youssef, C. M., & Luthans, F. (2007). Positive organizational behavior in the workplace – The impact of hope, optimism, and resilience. *Journal of Management*, 33(5), 774–800. doi: 10.1177/0149206307305562.

Zautra, A. J., & Reich, J. W. (2010). Resilience: The Meanings, Methods, and Measures of Human Adaptation. *The Oxford Handbook of Stress, Health, and Coping*, 173. Oxford University Press, New York.

Zorrilla E. P., DeRubeis R. J., & Redei, E. (1995). High self-esteem, hardiness and affective stability are associated with higher basal pituitary-adrenal hormone levels. *Psychoneuroendocrinology*, 20(6), 591–601. doi: 10.1016/0306-4530(95)00005-9.

Acknowledgements

Thank you to all those who have supported, encouraged and inspired me.

To Professor Patricia Riddell and Dr Dorota Bourne, both of whom have supported me through my research and taught me so much.

To my family, my mum and especially my sister Karen and step-mum Julie whom I cajoled into reading each draft chapter. Thank you both for your eye for detail and constructive feedback.

And to my friends, Sean, Tracy, Jo, Grace, Wendy and my oldest friend Gilly, who always believed in me, even when I didn't.

Finally, this book was partially funded using GoFundMe. Grateful thanks to those who contributed, especially Sean, Mark, Paula, Steve, Arthur, Sandra, Keren, Tim, Nick, Darren and all those who wanted to remain anonymous. You know who you are. Thank you.

The Author

Dr Sam Mather discovered neuroscience later in life, although she likes to describe it as her 'prime'. After decades of working in international organisations she has seen a change in the working landscape, not only from within organisations but also on the environment outside of work (not withstanding pandemics!). More than ever people need resilience. Her curiosity around what enables resilience led her to return to university to pursue her PhD in organisational psychology. This journey introduced her to neuroscience, which provided her with the 'how'. In understanding

the mechanisms of the brain that control how we feel
and behave, she was able to use science to explain
what happens to us when we have more demands
than we can deal with.

Armed with her three years of research, her knowledge of neuroscience, many years of experience in
industry and her sense of humour, Dr Sam has written this book for anyone who wants to increase their
personal toolkit for maintaining resilience and mental
well-being in or outside of work.

Dr Sam Mather has gained her experience across four
continents, in a range of industries, supporting organisations with their employee development, change
management, HR practices, diversity and inclusion,
and recruitment. She is also a qualified coach, neuroscience practitioner, NLP practitioner, and entertaining speaker. She currently lives in Berkshire in the UK.

Other books written by Dr Sam include *RISE Together:
A leaders' guide to the science behind creating innovative,
engaged and resilient employees.*

🌐 www.drsammather.com

Printed in Great Britain
by Amazon

78279983R00129